uk

PHILIP'S STUDENT ATLAS

Published in Great Britain in 2009 by Philip's,
a division of Octopus Publishing Group Limited
(www.octopusbooks.co.uk)
2–4 Heron Quays, London E14 4JP
An Hachette UK Company
(www.hachettelivre.co.uk)

Printed in Hong Kong

Cartography by Philip's
First edition

Copyright © 2009 Philip's

HARDBACK EDITION
ISBN 978-0-540-09251-2
PAPERBACK EDITION
ISBN 978-0-540-09252-9

SUBJECT LIST

Details of other Philip's titles and services can be found on our website at:
www.philips-maps.co.uk

MAP SYMBOLS

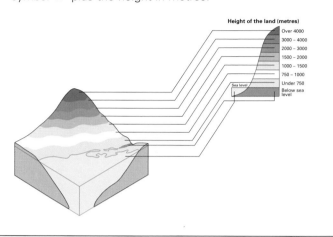

Sea
Coastline
Airport
Cape name
Colours showing the height of the land
Country name
River
National boundary (international boundaries are shown as ▬▬▬▬)
Lake
Line of longitude
High point, with height in metres
River name
Name of mountain range
Regional name
Main railway
Main road
Sea feature name
Line of latitude
Symbols locating towns: the larger the population of the town, the larger the symbol

HEIGHT OF LAND

There is an explanation like this one on every page where different colours are used to show the height of the land above sea level.

The highest point in a region is shown with the symbol ▲ plus the height in metres.

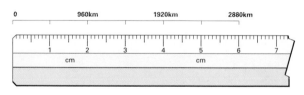

Height of the land (metres)

Over 4000
3000 – 4000
2000 – 3000
1500 – 2000
1000 – 1500
750 – 1000
Under 750
Below sea level

Sea level

SCALE BAR

Every map has a scale statement, scale bar and ruler accompanying it. For a full explanation of scale and how to use the scale bar, see page 2.

Scale 1:48 000 000   1 cm on the map = 480 km on the ground

0	960km	1920km	2880km

cm   cm

SCALE COMPARISON MAP

This map, or one of the U.K. and Ireland, appears on most of the maps of the continents at the same scale as the main map. They give an idea of the size of that continent.

England and Wales on same scale

LOCATOR MAP

There is a small map such as this on every map page. The dark green area shows how the main map fits into its larger region.

Philip's World Atlases are published in association with The Royal Geographical Society (with The Institute of British Geographers).

The Society was founded in 1830 and given a Royal Charter in 1859 for 'the advancement of geographical science'. Today it is a leading world centre for geographical learning – supporting education, teaching, research and expeditions, and promoting public understanding of the subject.

Further information about the Society and how to join may be found on its website at: **www.rgs.org**

PHOTOGRAPHIC ACKNOWLEDGEMENTS
© PTS Ltd p.6
© Patricia and Angus Macdonald p.7
© Crown Copyright p.7 (map extract)
© Fugro NPA Ltd, Edenbridge, Kent, UK (www.satmaps.co.uk) p.6, p.8, p.9, p.10, p.11, p.26, p.27, p.37, p.45, p.49, p.53, p.60, p.61, p.65, p.74, p.78, p.79
© iStockphoto.com p.22
© Eurostar p.24
© Corbis/Royalty Free p.73
© Fotolia.co.uk p.76

TYPES OF SCALE

In this atlas the scale of the map is shown in three ways:

WRITTEN STATEMENT

This tells you how many kilometres on the Earth are represented by one centimetre on the map.

1 cm on the map = 20 km on the ground

RATIO

This tells you that one unit on the map represents two million of the same unit on the ground.

1:2 000 000

SCALE BAR

This shows you the scale as a line or bar with a section of ruler beneath it.

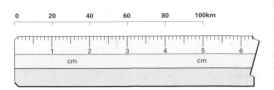

HOW TO MEASURE DISTANCE

The map on the right is a small part of the map of Southern Europe, which is on page 34 in the World section of the atlas.

The scale of the map extract is shown below:

Scale 1:10 000 000   1 cm on the map = 100 km on the ground

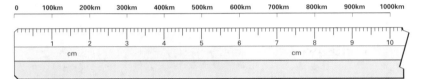

To measure the distance from London to Paris you can use any of the three methods described above.

For example:

USING THE WRITTEN STATEMENT

Using the scale above, you can see that 1 cm on the map represents 100 km on the ground.

Measure the distance on the map between London and Paris. You will see that this is about 3.5 cm.

If 1 cm = 100 km

then 3.5 cm = 350 km (3.5 × 100)

USING THE RATIO

Using the scale above, you can see that the ratio is 1:10 000 000.

We know that the distance on the map between the cities is 3.5 cm and we know from the ratio that 1 cm on the map = 10 000 000 cm on the ground. We multiply the map distance by the ratio.

= 3.5 × 10 000 000 cm
= 35 000 000 cm
= 350 000 m
= 350 km

USING THE SCALE BAR

We know that the distance on the map between the cities is 3.5 cm.

Using the scale bar, measure 3.5 cm along this (or use the ruler as a guide) and read off the distance.

Using these three methods, now work out the distance between London and Birmingham on the map above.

The map on the left is an extract from the map of Asia on page 40 in the World section of the atlas. Below, you can see the scale of this map. See if you can calculate the distance between Kolkata (Calcutta) and Bangkok.

Scale 1:48 000 000   1 cm on the map = 480 km on the ground

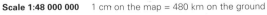

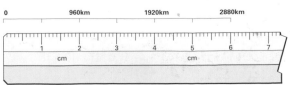

DIFFERENT SIZES OF SCALE

The table on the right shows the distances from London to Paris and Bangkok to Kolkata on the maps on page 2. The map distances are both 3.5 cm, but the actual distances are very different. This is because the maps are at different scales.

Included on most of the continent maps, in the World section of this atlas, are **scale comparison maps**. These show you the size of the UK and Ireland, or England and Wales, drawn at the same scale as the main map on that page. This is to give you an idea of the size of that continent.

	Map Distance	Scale	Actual Distance
London – Paris	3.5 cm	1:10 000 000	350 km
Bangkok – Kolkata	3.5 cm	1:48 000 000	1,680 km

Below are three maps which appear in this atlas:

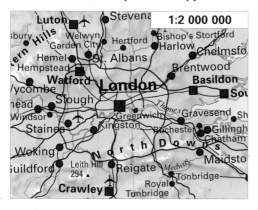

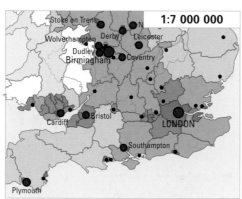

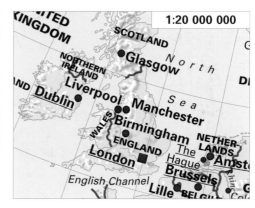

These maps all show London, but the map above shows much more detail than the maps on the right. The map above is a larger-scale map than the maps on the right.

A **large-scale** map shows more detail of a **small** area.

A **small-scale** map shows less detail of a **large** area.

Notice how the ratios are getting larger as the scale of the map gets smaller.

DIRECTION ON THE MAPS

On most of the atlas maps, north is at the top of the page. Longitude lines run from south to north. These usually curve a little because the Earth is a globe and not a flat shape.

POINTS OF THE COMPASS

Below is a drawing of the points of a compass. North, east, south and west are called **cardinal points**. Direction is sometimes given in degrees. This is measured clockwise from north. To help you remember the order of the compass points, try to learn this sentence:

Naughty **E**lephants **S**quirt **W**ater

USING A COMPASS

Compasses have a needle with a magnetic tip. The tip is attracted towards the Magnetic North Pole, which is close to the North Pole. The compass tells you where north is. You can see the Magnetic North Pole on the diagram below.

Look at the map of England and Wales on pages 12–13:

ACTIVITIES

Look at the map below.
If Ambleside is east of Belfast then:
• Valencia is _____ of Belfast;
• Renfrew is _____ of Ambleside;
• Oxford is _____ of Plymouth.
Look at the map of England and Wales on pages 12–13:
• Which is the most southerly town shown in England?
• Which is the most westerly town shown in Wales?

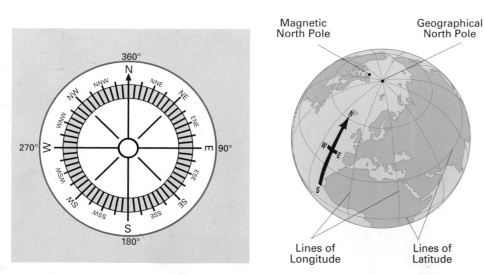

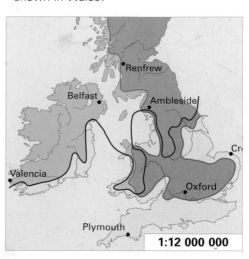

Latitude and Longitude

LATITUDE

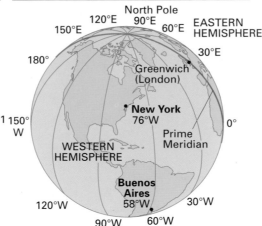

NORTHERN HEMISPHERE
North Pole 90°N
80°N
40°N — 40°N
60°N
20°N — New York 42°N — 20°N
0° — 0°
Equator
20°S — Buenos Aires 34°S — 20°S
SOUTHERN HEMISPHERE

Lines of latitude cross the atlas maps from east to west. The **Equator** is at 0°. All other lines of latitude are either north of the Equator, or south of the Equator. Line 40°N is almost halfway towards the North Pole. The North Pole is at 90°N. At the Equator, a degree of longitude measures about 110 km.

LONGITUDE

North Pole
120°E 90°E 60°E
150°E
EASTERN HEMISPHERE
180° 30°E
Greenwich (London)
1 150° W
New York 76°W
0°
Prime Meridian
WESTERN HEMISPHERE
Buenos Aires 58°W
120°W 30°W
90°W 60°W

Lines of longitude run from north to south. These lines meet at the North Pole and the South Pole. Longitude 0° passes through Greenwich. This line is also called the Prime Meridian. Lines of longitude are either east of 0° or west of 0°. There are 180 degrees of longitude both east and west of 0°.

USING LATITUDE AND LONGITUDE

New York 42°N 76°W

Buenos Aires 34°S 58°W

There are 60 minutes in a degree. Latitude and longitude lines make a grid. You can find a place if you know its latitude and longitude number. The latitude number is either north or south of the Equator. The longitude number is either east or west of the Greenwich Meridian.

SPECIAL LATITUDE LINES

The Earth's axis is tilted at an angle of approximately 23½°. In June, the northern hemisphere is tilted towards the Sun. On 21 June the Sun is directly overhead at the **Tropic of Cancer**, 23°26'N, and this is midsummer in the northern hemisphere. Midsummer in the southern hemisphere occurs on 21 December, when the Sun is overhead at the **Tropic of Capricorn**, 23°26'S. On the maps in this atlas these are shown as blue dotted lines.

In the North and South Polar regions there are places where the Sun does not rise or set above the horizon at certain times of the year. These places are also shown by a blue dotted line on the maps. The **Arctic Circle** is at 66°34'N and the **Antarctic Circle** is at 66°34'S.

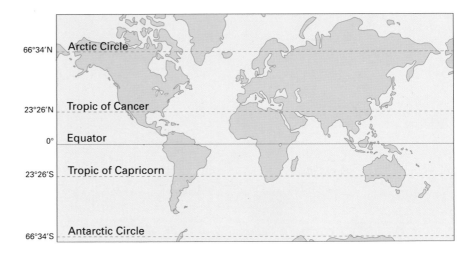

66°34'N — Arctic Circle
23°26'N — Tropic of Cancer
0° — Equator
23°26'S — Tropic of Capricorn
66°34'S — Antarctic Circle

LATITUDE AND LONGITUDE IN THIS ATLAS

In this atlas lines of latitude and longitude are coloured blue.

On large-scale maps, such as those of England and Wales on pages 12–13, there is a line for every degree. On smaller-scale maps only every other, every fifth or even tenth line is shown.

The map on the right shows the UK and Ireland. The latitude and longitude lines are numbered at the edges of the map. The bottom of the map shows whether a place is east or west of Greenwich. The side of the map tells you how far north from the Equator the line is.

Around the edges of the map are small yellow pointers with letters and figures in their boxes. Columns made by longitude lines have letters in their boxes; rows made by latitude lines have figures.

In the index at the end of the atlas, places have figure-letter references as well as latitude and longitude numbers to help you locate the place names on the maps.

On the map opposite, London is in rectangle **8M** (this is where row 8 crosses with column M). Edinburgh is in **4J** and Dublin is in **6F**.

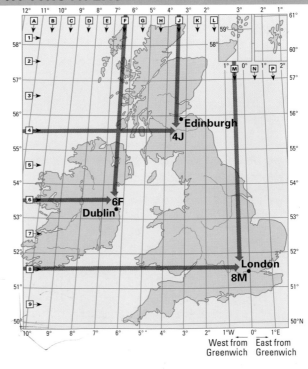

Edinburgh 4J
Dublin 6F
London 8M

West from Greenwich   East from Greenwich

HOW TO FIND A PLACE

The map on the right is an extract from the map of
Scotland on page 14. If you want to find Stornoway
in the atlas, you must look in the index. Places are
listed alphabetically. You will find the following entry:

Stornoway .... 58° 13'N 6° 23'W **14 1B**

The first number in **bold** type is the page number where the
map appears. The figure and letter which follow the page
number give the grid rectangle on the map in which the
feature appears. Here we can see that Stornoway is on
page 14 in the rectangle where row 1 crosses column B.

The latitude and longitude number corresponds with
the numbered lines on the map. The first set of figures
represent the latitude and the second set represent the
longitude. The unit of measurement for latitude and
longitude is the degree (°) which is divided into minutes (').

Latitude and longitude can be used to locate places
more accurately on smaller-scale maps such as those
in the World section. A more detailed expanation of
how to estimate the minutes can be found on page 90.

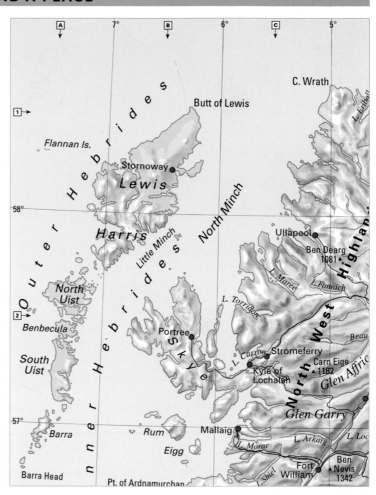

MAKING MAPS

One of the greatest problems in making maps is how to
draw the curved surface of the globe on a flat piece of paper.
As a globe is three dimensional, it is not possible to show
its surface on a flat map without some form of distortion.

This map (right) shows one way of putting the globe on
to paper, but because it splits up the land and sea it is not
very useful.

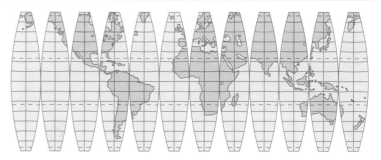

The map below is better because it shows the correct size of
places. It is an **equal-area map**. For example, Australia is the
correct size in relation to North America, and Europe is the
correct size in relation to Africa. Comparing certain areas is a
useful way to check the accuracy of maps. Comparing
Greenland (2.2 million km²) with Australia (7.7 million km²)
is a good 'area test'.

The map below is called **Mercator**. It has been used since the
16th century. The area scale is not equal area, but many sea
and air routes are drawn on this type of map because direction
is accurate. The scale of distances is difficult to put on a world
map. On the Mercator map, scale is correct along the Equator
but is less correct towards the Poles.

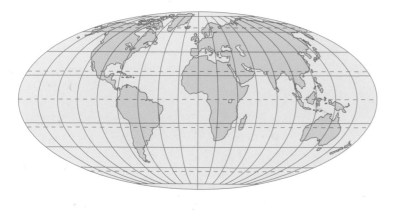

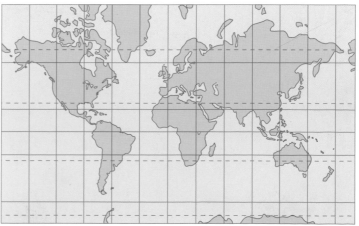

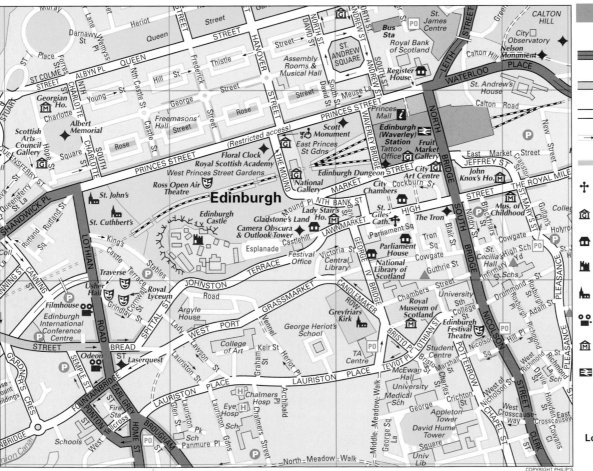

KEY TO MAP SYMBOLS

Main Road Dual		Shopping Street	
Secondary Road Single		Railway	
Minor Road		Railway / Bus Station	
One Way Street		Shopping Precinct / Retail Park	
Pedestrian Roads		Park	
✝ Abbey/Cathedral		🎭 Theatre	
Art Gallery		Tourist Information Centre	
Building of Public Interest		◆ Other Place of Interest	
Castle		H Hospital	
Church of interest		P Parking	
Cinema		PO Post Office	
Museum		▲ Youth Hostel	
Railway Station			

Scale 1:10 000   1 cm on the map and aerial photograph = 100 metres on the ground

0 ——————————— 500 metres ——————————— 1 km

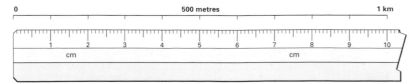

Locator map

Edinburgh

St Ives

COPYRIGHT PHILIP'S

KEY TO MAP SYMBOLS

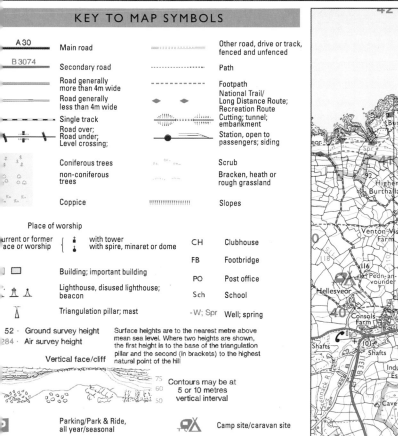

A 30	Main road
B 3074	Secondary road
	Road generally more than 4m wide
	Road generally less than 4m wide
	Single track
	Road over; Road under; Level crossing;
	Coniferous trees
	non-coniferous trees
	Coppice

Place of worship

current or former place or worship — with tower / with spire, minaret or dome

CH Clubhouse
FB Footbridge
PO Post office
Sch School
W; Spr Well; spring

Building; important building

Lighthouse, disused lighthouse; beacon

Triangulation pillar; mast

52 · Ground survey height
284 · Air survey height

Surface heights are to the nearest metre above mean sea level. Where two heights are shown, the first height is to the base of the triangulation pillar and the second (in brackets) to the highest natural point of the hill

Vertical face/cliff

Contours may be at 5 or 10 metres vertical interval

Other road, drive or track, fenced and unfenced

Path

Footpath

National Trail/ Long Distance Route; Recreation Route

Cutting; tunnel; embankment

Station, open to passengers; siding

Scrub

Bracken, heath or rough grassland

Slopes

Parking/Park & Ride, all year/seasonal

Information centre, all year/seasonal

Museum

Camp site/caravan site

Recreation/leisure/ sports centre

Golf course or links

Reproduced from the 2008 Ordnance Survey 1:25,000 Explorer Map with permission of the controller of Her Majesty's Stationery office © Crown Copyright

Scale of photograph 1:10 000

0 ————————— 500 metres

1 cm on the photograph = 100 metres on the ground

Scale of map 1:25 000

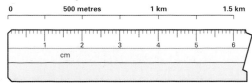

0 —— 500 metres —— 1 km —— 1.5 km

1 cm on the map = 250 metres on the ground

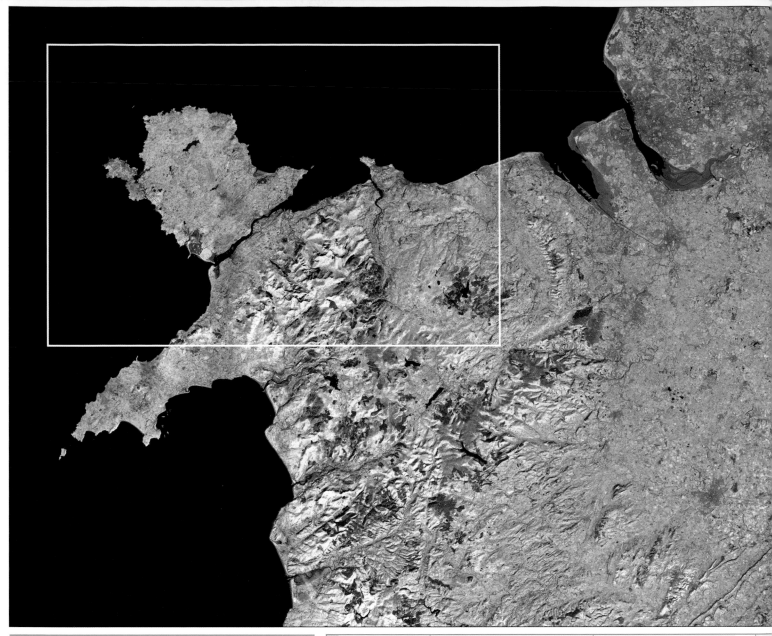

KEY TO MAP SYMBOLS

◉◉◉◉◎◉ ◦ ◦   Town symbols

⬡ Built-up areas	———	Main passenger railways
CONWY Administrative area names	———	Other passenger railways
SNOWDONIA National park names	⊕	Major airports
═══ Motorways	⌇	Rivers
━━━ Major roads	▱	Lakes or reservoirs
─── Other important roads	▲ 1085	Elevations in metres
─── Administrative boundaries	■	Places of interest

Locator map

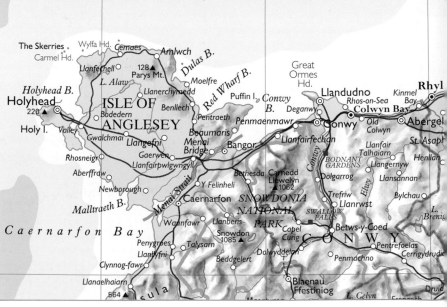

Scale 1:760 000   1 cm on the map and satellite image = 7.6 km on the ground

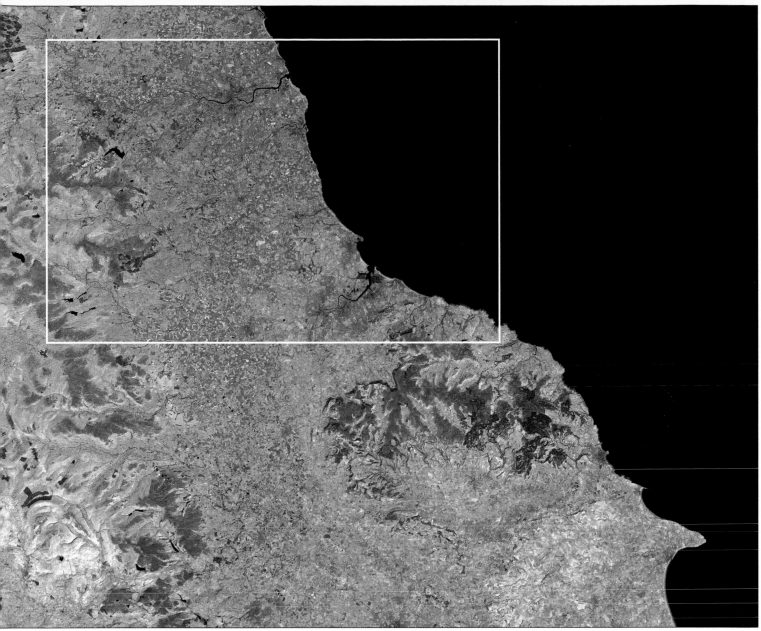

SATELLITE IMAGERY

e images on these pages were produced by the
ndsat 7 satellite, launched by NASA in 1999.
travels around the Earth at a height of over
0 km. It is able to scan every part of the Earth's
rface once every 16 days. The data is
nsmitted back to Earth where it is printed in
se colours to make certain features stand out.
On these pages grass and crops appear light
een, soils and exposed rock light grey, woodland
rk green, moorland brown, water black and
ilt-up areas dark grey. The image on this page
ows North-east England and the image on page
hows North Wales. Both images were
corded in late March. Comparing the maps,
nich are taken from *Philip's Modern School Atlas*
th the images helps identify specific features on
e images.

Locator map

Scale 1:760 000   1 cm on the map and satellite image = 7.6 km on the ground

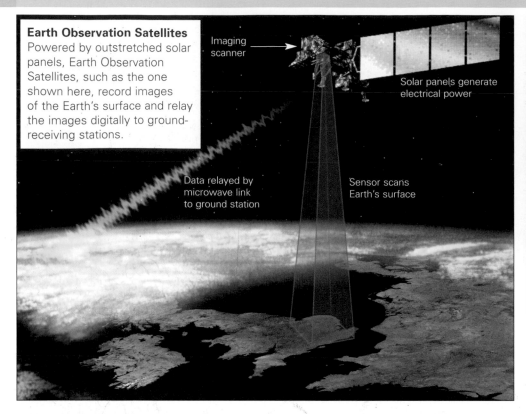

Earth Observation Satellites
Powered by outstretched solar panels, Earth Observation Satellites, such as the one shown here, record images of the Earth's surface and relay the images digitally to ground-receiving stations.

Imaging scanner

Solar panels generate electrical power

Data relayed by microwave link to ground station

Sensor scans Earth's surface

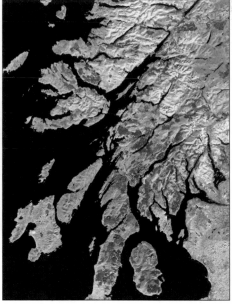

▲ **Western Scotland**
The rugged coastline of part of the west coast of Scotland is shown in this image. The long finger of land running north from the bottom of the image is the Mull of Kintyre, with the island of Arran to its right and the Firth of Clyde beyond.

◄ **Southern England**
This image shows parts of the counties of Hampshire and West Sussex with the Isle of Wight on the left, separated from the mainland by the Solent. The major towns of Southampton (far left), Portsmouth and Brighton are clearly visible along the coast, all appearing as purple.

▲ **The Thames Basin and London**
The River Thames, flowing from west to east, stands out in this image, which stretches from Richmond in the west, downstream to Erith in the east. Despite having a population of over 8 million people, there are still many parks and open spaces around the city centre which can be seen. The river joining the Thames from the north (centre right) is the River Lee. This flows through Stratford, the principal site for the 2012 Olympic Games.

▼ **The United Kingdom and Ireland, seen from Space**

The colours on this image have been processed to match the natural tone of the landscape. The large amount of agricultural land in the UK is reflected by the extensive green on the image. In Scotland, the snow-covered Cairngorm Mountains can be seen, with brownish-green coniferous forests below the snow line. Most of Ireland has a mid-green colour, which indicates the presence of rich pasture. In the west, the lighter colour indicates moorland or bare rock and is also visible in the Cambrian Mountains in Wales, the Pennines and the Lake District in England, and the Scottish Highlands. Urban areas are shown as purple in colour.

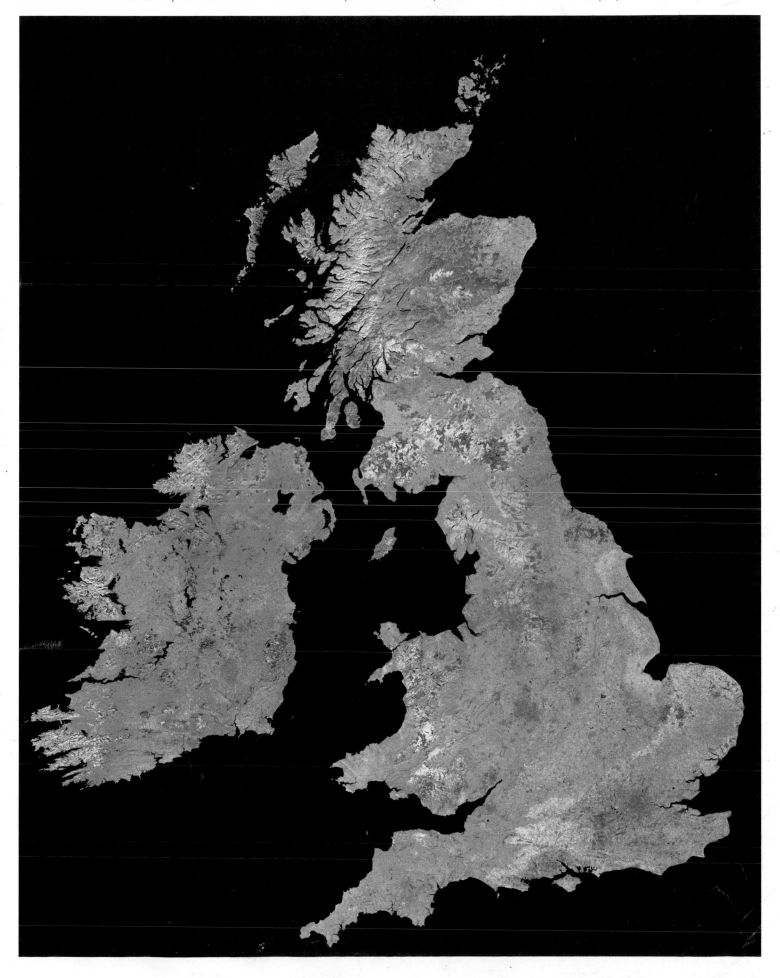

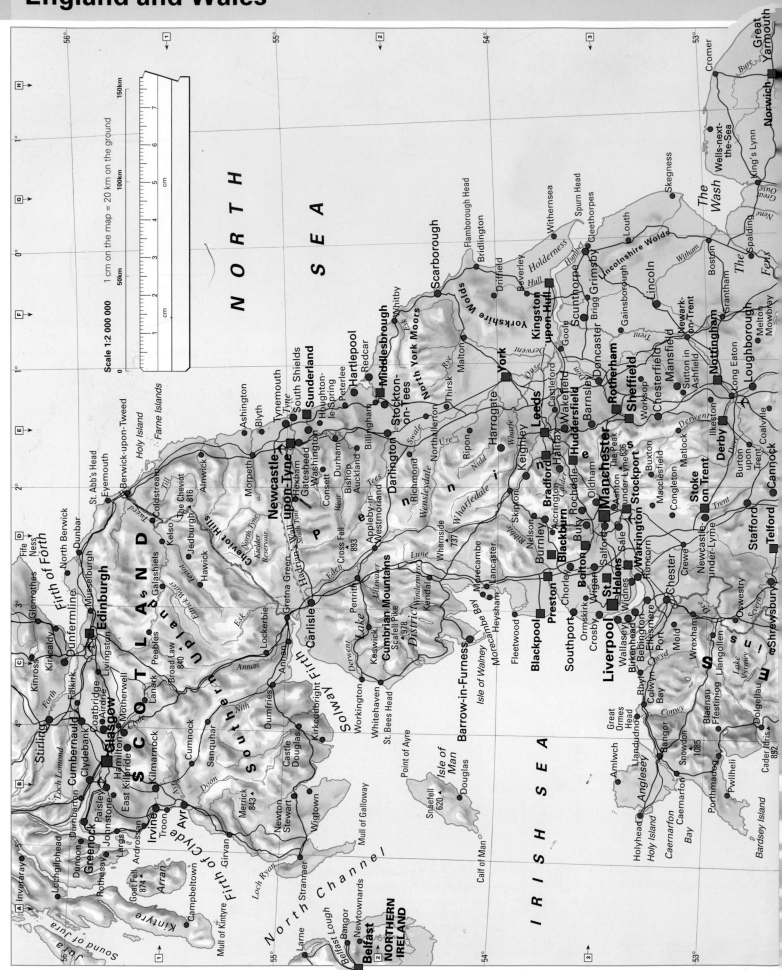

Scale 1:2 000 000   1 cm on the map = 20 km on the ground

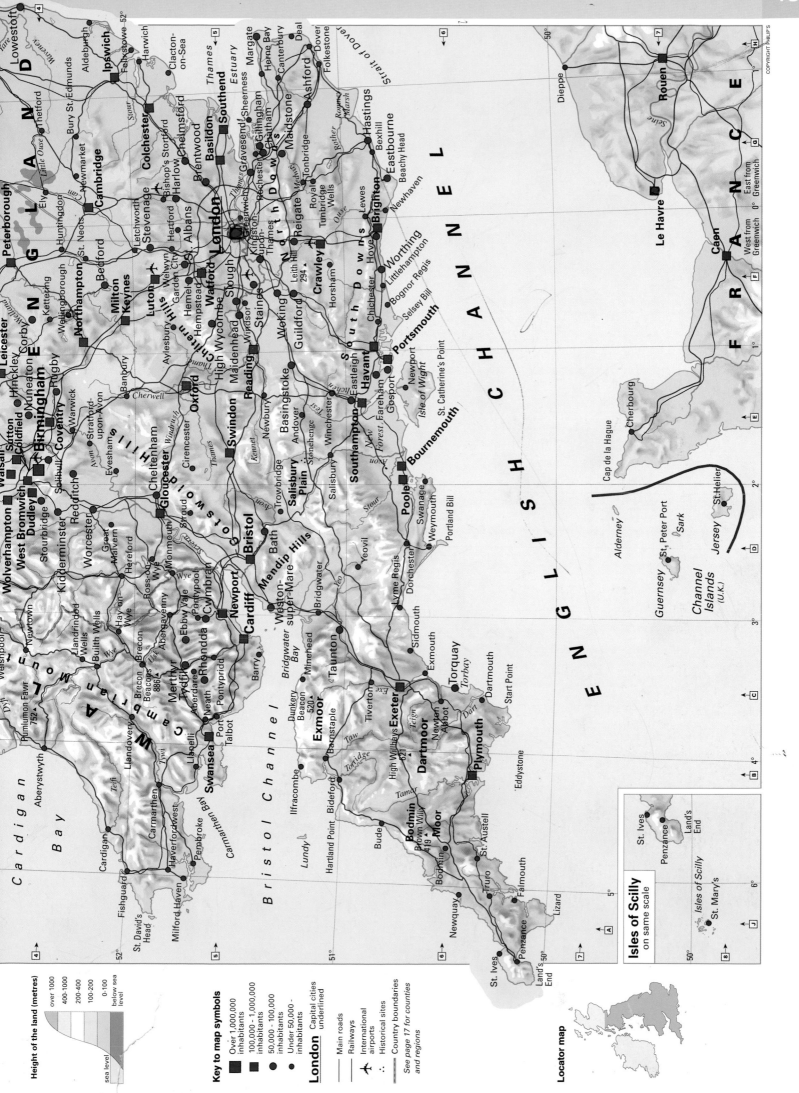

Height of the land (metres)

over 1000
400-1000
200-400
100-200
0-100
below sea level

sea level

Key to map symbols

Over 1,000,000 inhabitants
100,000 - 1,000,000 inhabitants
50,000 - 100,000 inhabitants
Under 50,000 inhabitants

London Capital cities underlined

Main roads
Railways
International airports
Historical sites
Country boundaries

See page 17 for counties and regions

Isles of Scilly
on same scale

St. Ives
Penzance
Land's End

Isles of Scilly
St. Mary's

Locator map

COPYRIGHT PHILIP'S

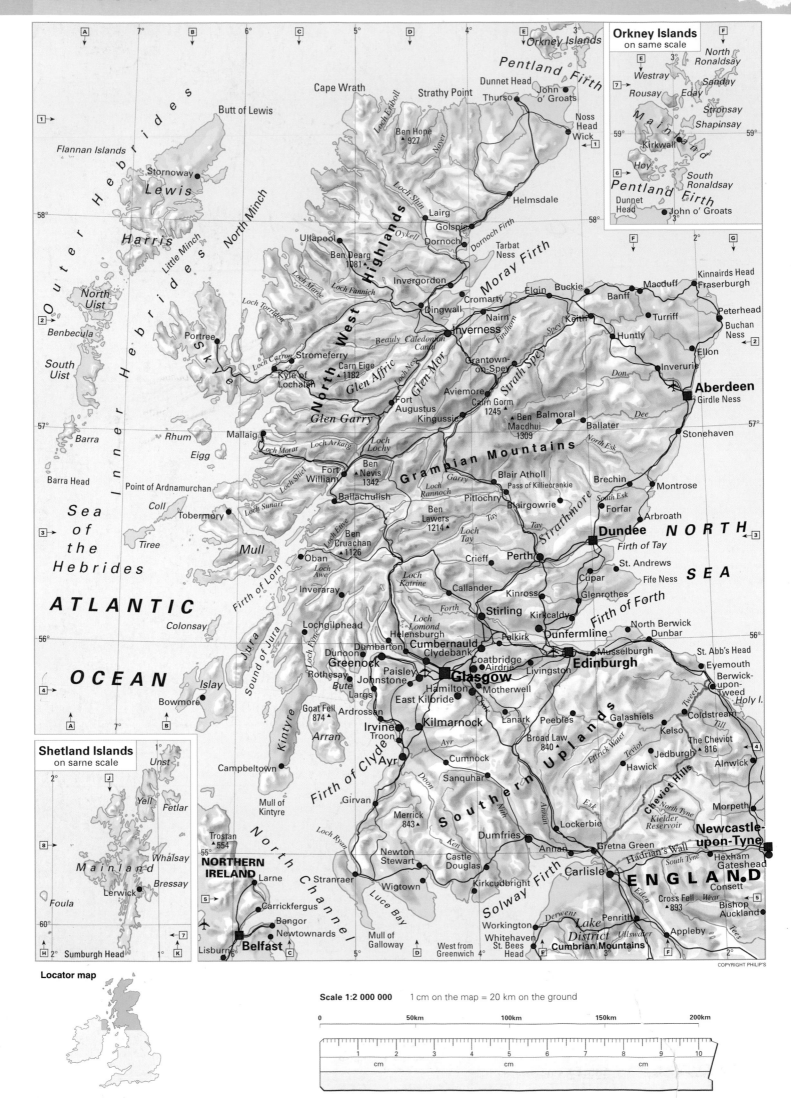

Orkney Islands
on same scale

Shetland Islands
on sarne scale

Locator map

Scale 1:2 000 000   1 cm on the map = 20 km on the ground

0   50km   100km   150km   200km

COPYRIGHT PHILIP'S

ATLANTIC

OCEAN

SCOTLAND
Campbeltown
Mull of Kintyre
Loch Ryan
Stranraer
Arran

North Channel

Malin Head
Tory Island
Inishowen Peninsula
Bloody Foreland
Giants Causeway
Rathlin Island
Ballycastle
Buncrana
Moville
Coleraine
Ballymena
Errigal 752▲
Lough Swilly
Ballymoney
Trostan ▲554
Mountains of Antrim
Letterkenny
Londonderry
Larne
Aran Island
Strabane
Carrickfergus
Rossan Point
Sperrin Mountains
Sawel 683
Antrim
Belfast Lough
Bangor
Donegal
Omagh
Cookstown
Lough Neagh
Belfast
Newtownards
Killybegs
NORTHERN
Ballyshannon
Lisburn
Ards Peninsula
Donegal Bay
Bundoran
Lower Lough Erne
Dungannon
IRELAND
Portadown
Lurgan
Ballyquintin Point
Erris Head
Enniskillen
Upper Lough Erne
Monaghan
Armagh
Banbridge
Downpatrick
Mullet Peninsula
Sligo Bay
Sligo
Lough Allen
Belturbet
Cootehill
Newry
Slieve Donard 852▲
Mourne Mountains
Dundrum Bay
Killala Bay
Colooney
Cavan
Carrickmacross
Warrenpoint
Ballina
Lough Conn
Boyle
Carrick-on-Shannon
Monaghan
Louth
Dundalk
Achill Island
Castlebar
Charlestown
Carrick-macross
Dundalk Bay
Clare Island
Knock
Castlerea
Longford
Blackwater
Drogheda
Inishturk
Westport
Claremorris
Roscommon
An Uaimh
Balbriggan
Inishbofin
Mweelrea ▲819
Lough Mask
Ballinrobe
Lough Ree
Mullingar
Boyne
Swords
Clifden
Lough Corrib
Tuam
Athlone
Leinster
Ireland's Eye
Slyne Head
Connacht
Galway
Ballinasloe
Edenderry
Howth Head
Dublin
Inishmore
Galway Bay
Loughrea
Tullamore
Bog of Allen
Liffey
Dun Laoghaire
Aran Islands
Gort
IRELAND
Birr
Naas
Bray
Hags Head
Lough Derg
Roscrea
Port Laoise
Kildare
Poulaphouca Reservoir
Wicklow Mountains
Wicklow
Milltown Malbay
Ennis
Killaloe
Nenagh
Keeper Hill ▲694
Thurles
Athy
Lugnaquillia 926▲
Kilkee
Kilrush
Limerick
Carlow
Tullow
Mizen Head
Arklow
Loop Head
Tipperary
Cashel
Kilkenny
Mount Leinster 796▲
Gorey
Mouth of the Shannon
Listowel
Newcastle West
Galtymore 920▲
Caher
Carrick-on-Suir
Enniscorthy
Kerry Head
Tralee Bay
Munster
Clonmel
New Ross
Wexford
Branden Mountain ▲953
Tralee
Mitchelstown
Knockmealdown Mountains
Waterford
Rosslare
Dingle
Maine
Kanturk
Fermoy
Tramore
Carnsore Point
Dunmore Head
Macgillycuddy's Reeks ▲1041
Carrauntoohill
Mallow
Blackwater
Dungarvan
Hook Head
Saltee Islands
St. David's Head
Valencia Island
Cahersiveen
Kenmare
Blarney
Cork
Youghal
WALES
Castletown Bearhaven
Caha Mountains
Killarney
Boggeragh Mountains
West Passage
Cobh
Crow Head
Bantry
Bandon
Bantry Bay
Bear Island
Clonakilty
Old Head of Kinsale
Skibbereen
Clear Island
Fastnet Rock
Cape Clear

CELTIC SEA

St. George's Channel

IRISH SEA

West from Greenwich

COPYRIGHT PHILIP'S

Height of the land (metres)

over 1000
400-1000
200-400
100-200
0-100
sea level
below sea level

Key to map symbols

■ Over 1,000,000 inhabitants
■ 100,000 - 1,000,000 inhabitants
● 50,000 - 100,000 inhabitants
• Under 50,000 inhabitants
Dublin Capital cities underlined

— Main roads
— Railways
✈ International airports
▭▭ Country boundaries

See page 17 for counties and regions

Locator map

Scale 1:4 600 000   1 cm on the map = 46 km on the ground

0   100km   200km   300km   400km

Height of the land (metres)

over 1000
400-1000
200-400
100-200
0-100
sea level   below sea level

	Highest mountains
	Largest lakes
	Longest rivers

England
Scafell Pike	978m
Windermere	15km²
Thames	346km
Severn	354km

Wales
Snowdon	1085m
Trawsfynydd Lake	5km²
Tywi	109km
Severn	354km

Scotland
Ben Nevis	1342m
Loch Lomond	70km²
Tay	188km

Northern Ireland
Slieve Donard	852m
Lough Neagh	396km²
Bann	128.7km

Ireland
Carrauntoohill	1041m
Lough Corrib	176km²
Shannon	370km

Shetland Islands
Unst
Yell
Mainland
Fair Isle

Orkney Islands
Westray
Sanday
Mainland
Hoy
Pentland Firth
Duncansby Head

Cape Wrath
Lewis
St. Kilda
Harris
North Uist
South Uist
Barra
Skye
Rhum
Coll
Tiree
Mull
Jura
Islay

Outer Hebrides
Inner Hebrides

North West Highlands
Dornoch Firth
Moray Firth
Kinnairds Head
Spey
Cairn Gorm 1245
Don
Dee
Grampian Mountains 1214
1182
Loch Ness
Ben Nevis 1342
Tay

ATLANTIC

OCEAN

Loch Lomond
Firth of Forth
Arran
Firth of Clyde
Malin Head
Rathlin Island
North Channel
Mull of Galloway
Solway Firth
Southern Uplands
843
Tweed
The Cheviot 816
840
St. Abbs Head
Holy Island

NORTH
Great Britain
SEA

Tyne
Pennines
893
Tees
North York Moors 454
Flamborough Head

752
Mourne 554
683
Bann
Lough Neagh
Donegal Bay
Lough Erne
644
852
Slieve Donard

Lake District
Scafell Pike 978
Windermere
Morecambe Bay
Isle of Man
Spurn Head

Ireland

IRISH SEA

Erris Head
Achill Island
819
Lough Corrib
Lough Ree
Boyne
Liverpool Bay
Aire
Ouse
Humber

Galway Bay
Aran Islands
Shannon
Liffey
Anglesey
Mersey
The Peak 636
Trent
The Wash
The Fens
Lowestoft Ness
Yare

Lough Derg
Wicklow Mountains 926
920
Barrow
Snowdon 1085
Trawsfynydd Lake
Dee
Severn
315
Nene
Ouse

Shannon
Blackwater
Suir
953
Lee
920
St. David's Head
Cardigan Bay
Cambrian Mountains
Wye
Avon
330
Chiltern Hills
Thames
North Foreland

Dingle Bay 1041
Carrauntoohill
Bantry Bay
Fastnet Rock
Cape Clear

St. George's Channel
Carmarthen Bay
Tywi
Brecon 886 Beacons
Severn
297
Cotswolds
Salisbury Plain
North Downs
South Downs
Beachy Head
Strait of Dover

CELTIC

SEA

Lundy
Bristol Channel
Exmoor
Hartland Point
Tamar
621 Dartmoor
Lyme Bay
Portland Bill
Isle of Wight

ENGLISH CHANNEL

Start Point
Isles of Scilly
Land's End
Lizard

Channel Islands
Guernsey
Jersey

France

West from Greenwich 0° East from Greenwich

COPYRIGHT PHILIP'S

COUNTRY FACTS

Country Name	Area (square kilometres)	Inhabitants (thousands 2007)	Capital City or Town
UNITED KINGDOM	**240,883**	**60,975**	**LONDON**
of which England	129,652	51,092	London
Wales	20,628	2,980	Cardiff
Scotland	77,097	5,144	Edinburgh
Northern Ireland	13,532	1,759	Belfast
*Isle of Man	572	76	Douglas
* Jersey	116	91	St. Helier
*Guernsey	63	66	St. Peter Port
IRELAND	**68,896**	**4,109**	**DUBLIN**

* Crown Dependencies which are not part of the U.K.

The map shows the 6 counties in Northern Ireland, the 32 unitary authorities in Scotland, the 22 unitary authorities in Wales and the 87 unitary authorities in England as of 1st April 2009. Authorities which are too small to name on the map are numbered and listed separately.

SCOTLAND
1. ABERDEEN CITY
2. DUNDEE CITY
3. WEST DUNBARTONSHIRE
4. EAST DUNBARTONSHIRE
5. CITY OF GLASGOW
6. INVERCLYDE
7. RENFREWSHIRE
8. EAST RENFREWSHIRE
9. NORTH LANARKSHIRE
10. FALKIRK
11. CLACKMANNANSHIRE
12. WEST LOTHIAN
13. CITY OF EDINBURGH
14. MIDLOTHIAN

● Capital cities

WALES
15. SWANSEA
16. NEATH PORT TALBOT
17. BRIDGEND
18. RHONDDA CYNON TAFF
19. MERTHYR TYDFIL
20. CAERPHILLY
21. BLAENAU GWENT
22. TORFAEN
23. CARDIFF
24. NEWPORT

ENGLAND
25. HARTLEPOOL
26. DARLINGTON
27. STOCKTON-ON-TEES
28. MIDDLESBROUGH
29. REDCAR AND CLEVELAND
30. BLACKPOOL
31. BLACKBURN WITH DARWEN
32. HALTON
33. WARRINGTON
34. KINGSTON UPON HULL
35. NORTH EAST LINCOLNSHIRE
36. STOKE-ON-TRENT
37. TELFORD AND WREKIN
38. DERBY CITY
39. CITY OF NOTTINGHAM
40. LEICESTER CITY
41. RUTLAND
42. PETERBOROUGH
43. MILTON KEYNES
44. LUTON
45. NORTH SOMERSET
46. CITY OF BRISTOL
47. BATH AND N. E. SOMERSET
48. SWINDON
49. READING
50. WOKINGHAM
51. WINDSOR AND MAIDENHEAD
52. SLOUGH
53. BRACKNELL FOREST
54. THURROCK
55. SOUTHEND-ON-SEA
56. MEDWAY
57. PLYMOUTH
58. TORBAY
59. POOLE
60. BOURNEMOUTH
61. SOUTHAMPTON
62. PORTSMOUTH
63. BRIGHTON AND HOVE
64. BEDFORD
65. CENTRAL BEDFORDSHIRE

The Channel Islands and the Isle of Man are dependencies of the Crown and have their own parliaments. They are not part of the United Kingdom.

Weather is measured in terms of rainfall, temperature, cloudiness, sunshine and wind over a short period of time, usually less than a day. Climate is the average of the weather over a longer period, usually 30 years.

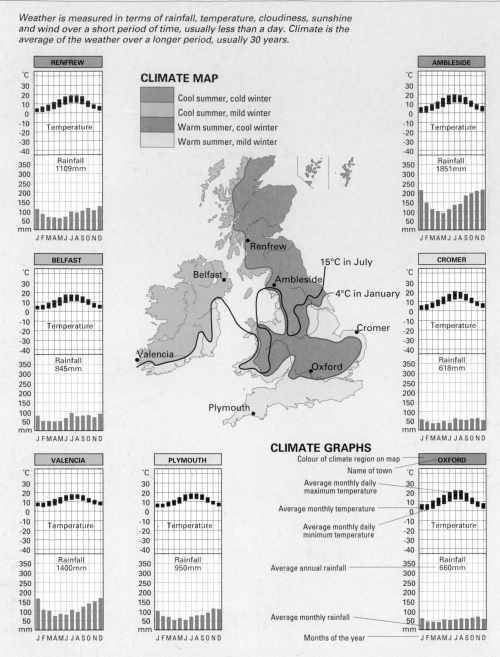

CLIMATE MAP

- Cool summer, cold winter
- Cool summer, mild winter
- Warm summer, cool winter
- Warm summer, mild winter

15°C in July
4°C in January

RENFREW
Temperature
Rainfall 1109mm

AMBLESIDE
Temperature
Rainfall 1851mm

BELFAST
Temperature
Rainfall 845mm

CROMER
Temperature
Rainfall 618mm

VALENCIA
Temperature
Rainfall 1400mm

PLYMOUTH
Temperature
Rainfall 950mm

CLIMATE GRAPHS

Colour of climate region on map
Name of town
Average monthly daily maximum temperature
Average monthly temperature
Average monthly daily minimum temperature
Average annual rainfall
Average monthly rainfall
Months of the year

OXFORD
Temperature
Rainfall 660mm

Renfrew
Belfast
Ambleside
Cromer
Valencia
Oxford
Plymouth

ANNUAL RAINFALL
Average annual rainfall

- 2000 millimetres
- 1000 millimetres
- 750 millimetres
- Prevailing winds

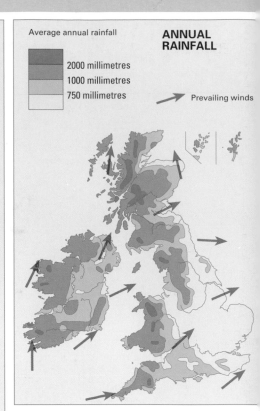

DAILY SUNSHINE
Average hours per day

- 4.5 hours
- 4 hours
- 3.5 hours
- 3 hours

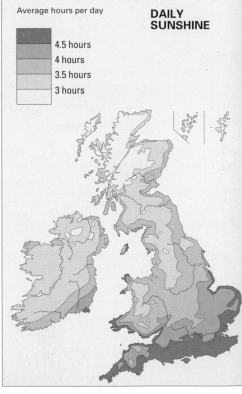

JANUARY TEMPERATURE
Average monthly temperature

- 6°C†
- 4°C
- 2°C
- 0°C*

Oban 416 — Average number of hours of sunshine November–April

* Freezing point
† Minimum temperature for plant growth

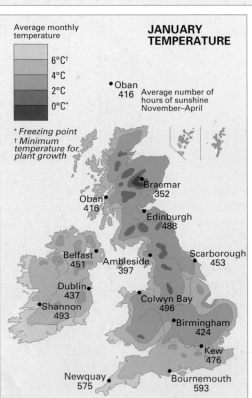

Oban 416
Braemar 352
Edinburgh 488
Belfast 451
Ambleside 397
Scarborough 453
Dublin 437
Shannon 493
Colwyn Bay 496
Birmingham 424
Kew 476
Newquay 575
Bournemouth 593

JULY TEMPERATURE
Average monthly temperature

- 16°C
- 14°C
- 12°C
- 10°C

Oban 825 — Average number of hours of sunshine May–October

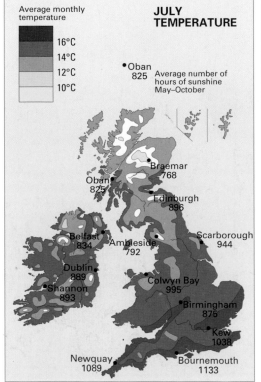

Oban 825
Braemar 768
Edinburgh 896
Belfast 834
Ambleside 792
Scarborough 944
Dublin 889
Shannon 893
Colwyn Bay 995
Birmingham 875
Kew 1038
Newquay 1089
Bournemouth 1133

Temperature Records
Highest
38.5°C Brogdale near Faversham, Kent, 10 August 2003
Lowest
-27.2°C Braemar, Aberdeenshire, 10 January 1982 and 11 February 1895, Altnaharra, Highland, 30 December 1995

Rainfall Records
Highest 24 hour total
279 mm Martinstown, near Dorchester, Dorset, 18 July 1955

Sunshine Records
Highest monthly total
384 hours Eastbourne and Hastings, Sussex, July 1911
Lowest monthly total
0 hours Westminster, Greater London, December 1890

Highest Gust Records
150 knots Cairngorm, 20 March 1986

COPYRIGHT PHILIP'S

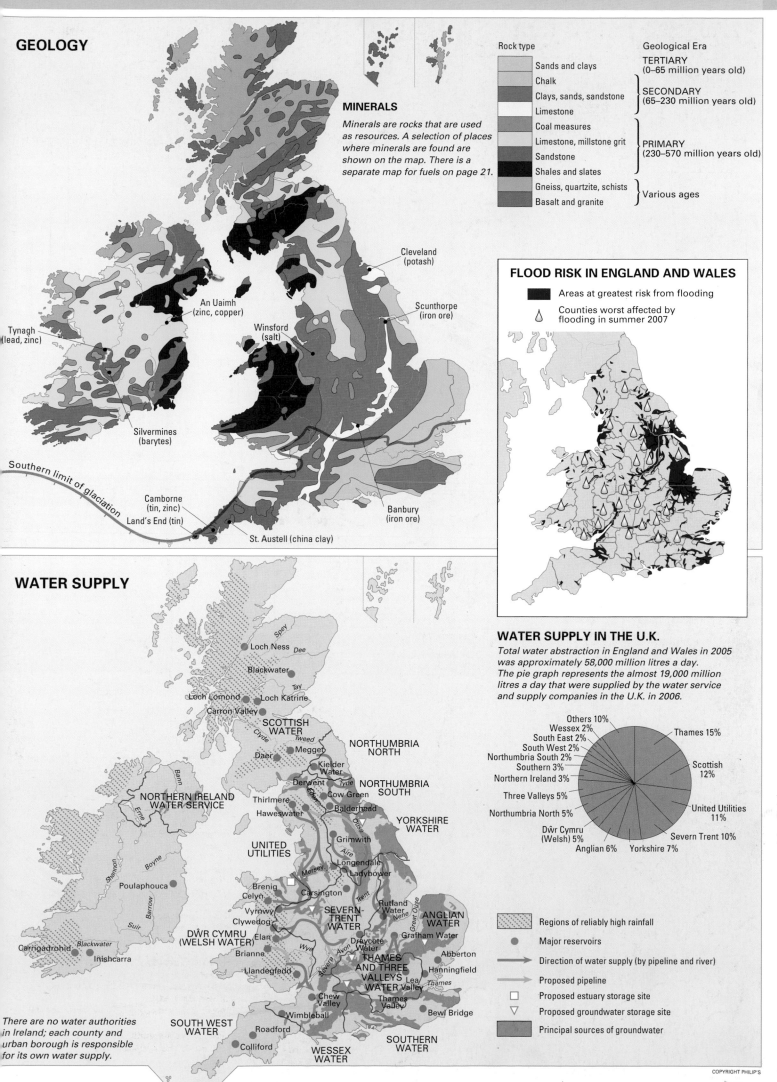

GEOLOGY

MINERALS

Minerals are rocks that are used as resources. A selection of places where minerals are found are shown on the map. There is a separate map for fuels on page 21.

Rock type — **Geological Era**

Rock type	Era
Sands and clays	TERTIARY (0–65 million years old)
Chalk	
Clays, sands, sandstone	SECONDARY (65–230 million years old)
Limestone	
Coal measures	
Limestone, millstone grit	PRIMARY (230–570 million years old)
Sandstone	
Shales and slates	
Gneiss, quartzite, schists	Various ages
Basalt and granite	

Cleveland (potash)

An Uaimh (zinc, copper)

Scunthorpe (iron ore)

Winsford (salt)

Tynagh (lead, zinc)

Silvermines (barytes)

Southern limit of glaciation

Camborne (tin, zinc)

Land's End (tin)

Banbury (iron ore)

St. Austell (china clay)

FLOOD RISK IN ENGLAND AND WALES

■ Areas at greatest risk from flooding

⬧ Counties worst affected by flooding in summer 2007

WATER SUPPLY

WATER SUPPLY IN THE U.K.

Total water abstraction in England and Wales in 2005 was approximately 58,000 million litres a day. The pie graph represents the almost 19,000 million litres a day that were supplied by the water service and supply companies in the U.K. in 2006.

Pie graph:
- Others 10%
- Wessex 2%
- South East 2%
- South West 2%
- Northumbria South 2%
- Southern 3%
- Northern Ireland 3%
- Three Valleys 5%
- Northumbria North 5%
- Dŵr Cymru (Welsh) 5%
- Anglian 6%
- Yorkshire 7%
- Severn Trent 10%
- United Utilities 11%
- Scottish 12%
- Thames 15%

Spey
Loch Ness   Dee
Blackwater
Tay
Loch Lomond   Loch Katrine
Carron Valley
SCOTTISH WATER
Clyde   Tweed
Megget
Daer   NORTHUMBRIA NORTH
Bann
Kielder Water
Derwent   Tyne   NORTHUMBRIA SOUTH
NORTHERN IRELAND WATER SERVICE   Cow Green
Thirlmere   Balderhead
Erne   Haweswater   YORKSHIRE WATER
Grimwith
UNITED UTILITIES   Aire
Boyne   Longendale
Shannon   Mersey   Ladybower
Poulaphouca   Brenig   Carsington   Trent
Celyn   SEVERN-   Rutland Water
Barrow   Vyrnwy   TRENT   Nene   Great Ouse
Suir   Clywedog   WATER   ANGLIAN WATER
DŴR CYMRU   Elan   Draycote   Grafham Water
Carrigadrohid   Blackwater   (WELSH WATER)   Water
Inishcarra   Brianne   Avon   Abberton
Llandegfedd   Wye   THAMES   Hanningfield
Severn   AND THREE   Thames
VALLEYS   Lea
WATER   Valley
Chew Valley   Thames Valley
Wimbleball   Valley
SOUTH WEST WATER   Bewl Bridge
Roadford   SOUTHERN WATER
Colliford   WESSEX WATER

There are no water authorities in Ireland; each county and urban borough is responsible for its own water supply.

Legend:
▨ Regions of reliably high rainfall
● Major reservoirs
→ Direction of water supply (by pipeline and river)
→ Proposed pipeline
□ Proposed estuary storage site
▽ Proposed groundwater storage site
▨ Principal sources of groundwater

COPYRIGHT PHILIP'S

TYPES OF FARM

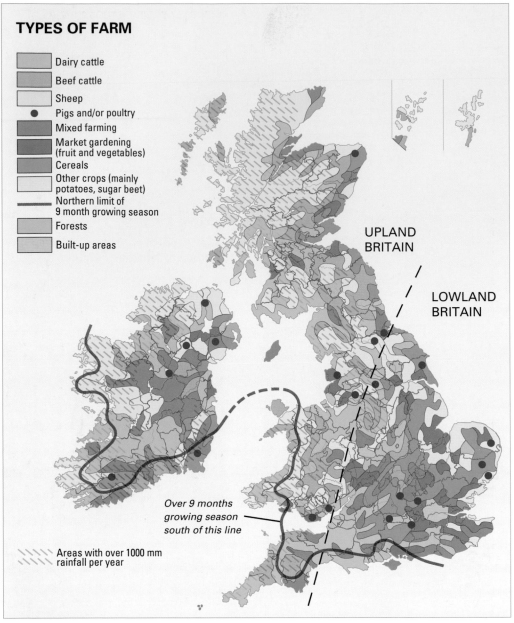

- Dairy cattle
- Beef cattle
- Sheep
- ● Pigs and/or poultry
- Mixed farming
- Market gardening (fruit and vegetables)
- Cereals
- Other crops (mainly potatoes, sugar beet)
- ▬ Northern limit of 9 month growing season
- Forests
- Built-up areas

UPLAND BRITAIN

LOWLAND BRITAIN

Over 9 months growing season south of this line

/// Areas with over 1000 mm rainfall per year

CEREAL FARMING

The percentage of the total farmland used for growing cereals in 2007

- Over 40%
- 30 – 40%
- 20 – 30%
- 10 – 20%
- 0 – 10%
- No data

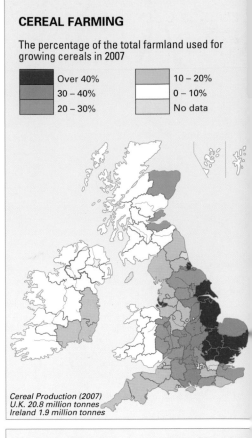

Cereal Production (2007)
U.K. 20.8 million tonnes
Ireland 1.9 million tonnes

DAIRY FARMING

The number of dairy cows per 100 hectares of farmland in 2007

- Over 40
- 30 – 40
- 20 – 30
- 10 – 20
- 0 – 10
- No data

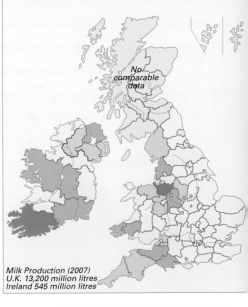

No comparable data

Milk Production (2007)
U.K. 13,200 million litres
Ireland 545 million litres

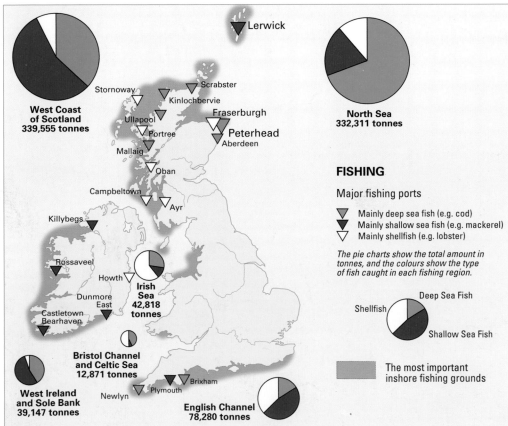

West Coast of Scotland 339,555 tonnes

▼ Lerwick

Stornoway
Scrabster
Kinlochbervie
Ullapool
Portree
Fraserburgh
Peterhead
Aberdeen
Mallaig
Oban
Campbeltown
Ayr

North Sea 332,311 tonnes

Killybegs
Rossaveel
Howth
Irish Sea 42,818 tonnes
Dunmore East
Castletown Bearhaven

Bristol Channel and Celtic Sea 12,871 tonnes

West Ireland and Sole Bank 39,147 tonnes

Newlyn
Plymouth
Brixham

English Channel 78,280 tonnes

FISHING

Major fishing ports

- ▽ Mainly deep sea fish (e.g. cod)
- ▼ Mainly shallow sea fish (e.g. mackerel)
- ▽ Mainly shellfish (e.g. lobster)

The pie charts show the total amount in tonnes, and the colours show the type of fish caught in each fishing region.

Deep Sea Fish
Shellfish
Shallow Sea Fish

The most important inshore fishing grounds

AGRICULTURAL LAND USE IN THE U.K.

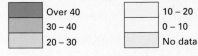

Other agricultural land 12.1%
Oats 0.6%
Sugar beet 0.8%
Potatoes 0.8%
Horticultural 1.0%
Rapeseed 3.2%
Barley 5.8%
Wheat 11.6%
Rough grazing 25.2%
Pasture 38.9%

Total agricultural land area (2005): 18.5 million hectares

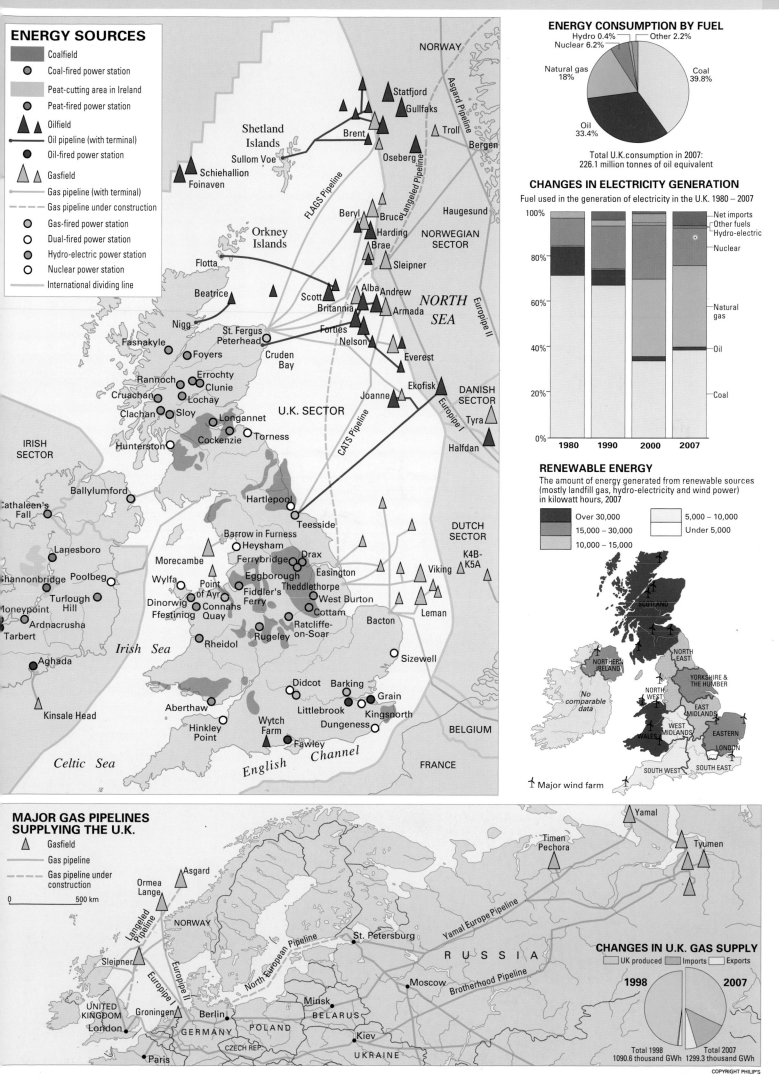

ENERGY SOURCES

- ▨ Coalfield
- ● Coal-fired power station
- ▨ Peat-cutting area in Ireland
- ● Peat-fired power station
- ▲ Oilfield
- ━ Oil pipeline (with terminal)
- ● Oil-fired power station
- △ Gasfield
- ━ Gas pipeline (with terminal)
- - - Gas pipeline under construction
- ● Gas-fired power station
- ○ Dual-fired power station
- ● Hydro-electric power station
- ○ Nuclear power station
- ━ International dividing line

ENERGY CONSUMPTION BY FUEL

Hydro 0.4%
Other 2.2%
Nuclear 6.2%
Natural gas 18%
Coal 39.8%
Oil 33.4%

Total U.K. consumption in 2007:
226.1 million tonnes of oil equivalent

CHANGES IN ELECTRICITY GENERATION

Fuel used in the generation of electricity in the U.K. 1980 – 2007

Net imports
Other fuels
Hydro-electric
Nuclear
Natural gas
Oil
Coal

1980 1990 2000 2007

RENEWABLE ENERGY

The amount of energy generated from renewable sources (mostly landfill gas, hydro-electricity and wind power) in kilowatt hours, 2007

- Over 30,000
- 15,000 – 30,000
- 10,000 – 15,000
- 5,000 – 10,000
- Under 5,000

↑ Major wind farm

MAJOR GAS PIPELINES SUPPLYING THE U.K.

- △ Gasfield
- ━ Gas pipeline
- - - Gas pipeline under construction

0 ___ 500 km

CHANGES IN U.K. GAS SUPPLY

UK produced | Imports | Exports

1998   2007

Total 1998   Total 2007
1090.6 thousand GWh   1299.3 thousand GWh

COPYRIGHT PHILIP'S

All types of work can be divided into three groups:
1. *Industry which produces raw materials. This includes farming, forestry, fishing, mining, energy and water supply.*
2. *Industry which manufactures goods out of raw materials. This includes metals, chemicals, engineering and textiles.*
3. *Industry which provides services not goods. This includes work in offices, tourism, transport, construction and government.*

EMPLOYMENT
SERVICES

The percentage of the workforce employed in the service industry in 2007

- Over 85% in services
- 80% – 85% in services
- 75% – 80% in services
- 70% – 75% in services
- Under 70% in services

U.K. as a whole 75.3%
Ireland as a whole 36.0%

FARMING, FORESTRY AND FISHING

Indicates over 10% of the workforce employed in farming, forestry and fishing

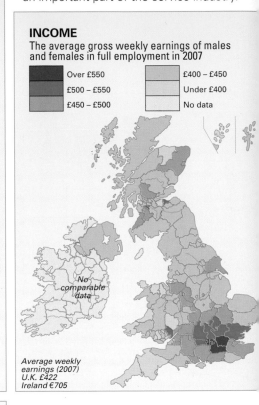

▲ Canary Wharf, London, is a centre of bankir – an important part of the service industry.

INCOME
The average gross weekly earnings of males and females in full employment in 2007

- Over £550
- £500 – £550
- £450 – £500
- £400 – £450
- Under £400
- No data

No comparable data

Average weekly earnings (2007)
U.K. £422
Ireland €705

EMPLOYMENT IN MANUFACTURING INDUSTRY

The percentage of the workforce employed in manufacturing in 2007

- Over 20%
- 16% – 20%
- 14% – 16%
- 12% – 14%
- 10% – 12%
- Under 10%

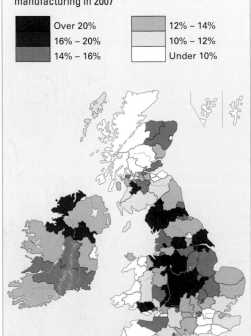

UNEMPLOYMENT

The percentage of the workforce unemployed in 2007

- Over 8%
- 7% – 8%
- 6% – 7%
- 5% – 6%
- 4% – 5%
- Under 4%

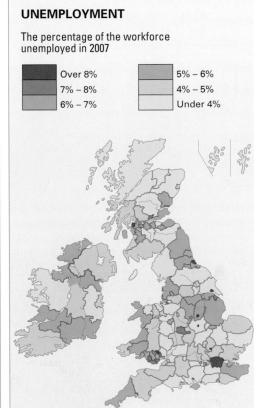

U.K. TRADE

Trade is balanced by money coming in for services such as banking and insurance.

Total Imports 2007
£267,317 million

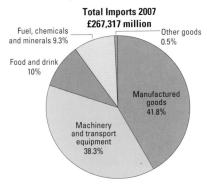

- Fuel, chemicals and minerals 9.3%
- Other goods 0.5%
- Food and drink 10%
- Manufactured goods 41.8%
- Machinery and transport equipment 38.3%

Total Exports 2007
£206,827 million

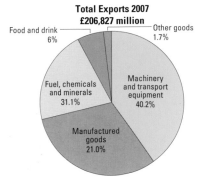

- Food and drink 6%
- Other goods 1.7%
- Fuel, chemicals and minerals 31.1%
- Machinery and transport equipment 40.2%
- Manufactured goods 21.0%

POPULATION FACTS

U.K. Population 2007	60,975,000
of which England	51,092,000
Scotland	5,144,000
Wales	2,980,000
Northern Ireland	1,759,000
Ireland Population 2007	4,109,000

AGE STRUCTURE OF THE U.K. IN 1901 AND 2007

The age structure shows how old people are and the percentage in each age group that is male and female. The diagram is called a population pyramid. For example, in 1901, 20% of the female population was aged between 10–19. In 2007, about 12% were in this group.

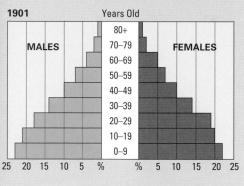

POPULATION DENSITY

Number of people per square kilometre in 2007

- Over 1000
- 500 – 1000
- 200 – 500
- 100 – 200
- 50 – 100
- 25 – 50
- Under 25

The average density for the U.K. is 251 people per km². The average density for the Republic of Ireland is 61 people per km².

Population of major cities

- Over 5,000,000
- 1,000,000 – 5,000,000
- 400,000 – 1,000,000
- 200,000 – 400,000
- 100,000 – 200,000

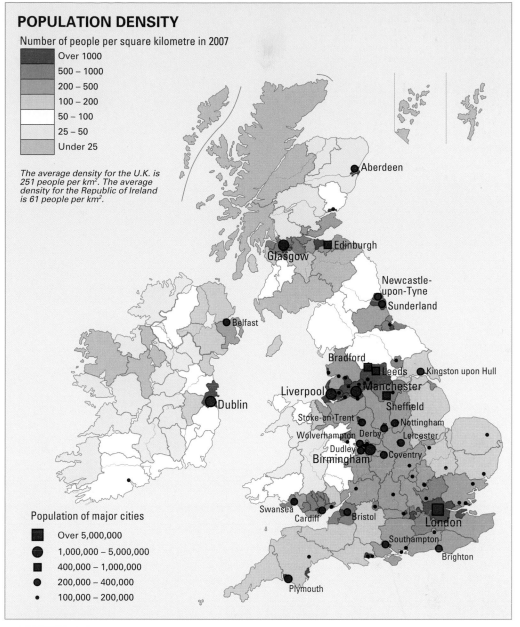

ETHNIC GROUPS

Ethnic minorities as a % of total population in 2003

- Over 30%
- 10 – 30%
- 5 – 10%
- 0 – 5%

Ethnic minority groups

- 10mm = 150,000 people
- Indian/ Pakistani/ Bangladeshi
- W. Indian/ African
- Other

77,000   Total number of ethnic minority people in each region

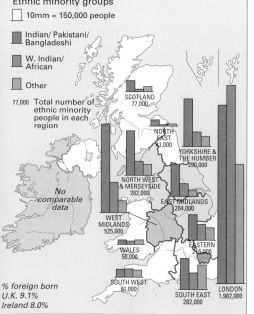

SCOTLAND 77,000
NORTH EAST 91,000
YORKSHIRE & THE HUMBER 290,000
NORTH WEST & MERSEYSIDE 282,000
EAST MIDLANDS 204,000
No comparable data
WEST MIDLANDS 525,000
EASTERN 216,000
WALES 50,000
SOUTH WEST 91,000
SOUTH EAST 282,000
LONDON 1,982,000

% foreign born
U.K. 9.1%
Ireland 8.0%

YOUNG PEOPLE

The percentage of the population under 15 years old in 2007

- Over 21%
- 20 – 21%
- 19 – 20%
- 18 – 19%
- 17 – 18%
- Under 17%

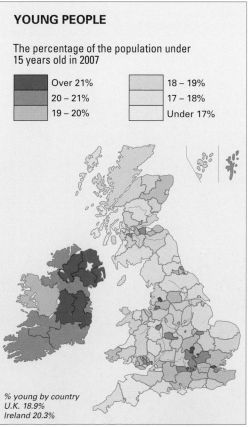

% young by country
U.K. 18.9%
Ireland 20.3%

OLD PEOPLE

The percentage of the population over pensionable age* in 2007

- Over 26%
- 24 – 26%
- 22 – 24%
- 20 – 22%
- 18 – 20%
- Under 18%

*Pensionable age is 65 for males, 60 for females

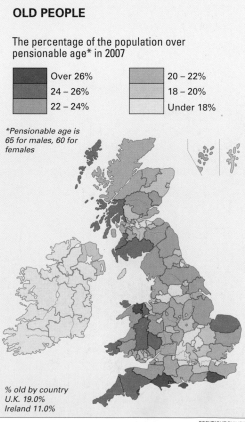

% old by country
U.K. 19.0%
Ireland 11.0%

ROADS AND FERRIES

- ▬M6▬ Motorways
- ──── Other main roads
- ········· Principal car ferry routes

RAILWAYS

- ──── Electrified lines
- ──── Other main lines
- ----- Channel Tunnel
- ──── High-speed rail link

The fastest journey time from London to Paris via the Channel Tunnel is now 2 hours 15 minutes, London to Brussels is 1 hour 51 minutes.

AIRPORTS

Passenger traffic in thousands (2007)

60,000
30,000
5,000
1,000

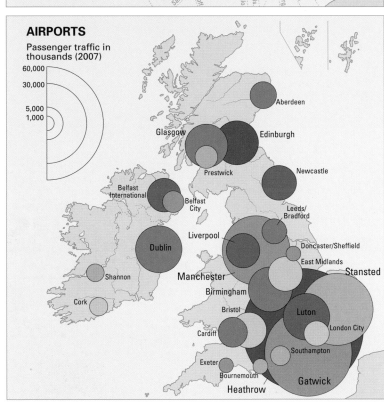

SEAPORTS

Goods traffic by port in thousand tonnes (2006)

50,000
25,000
10,000
5,000

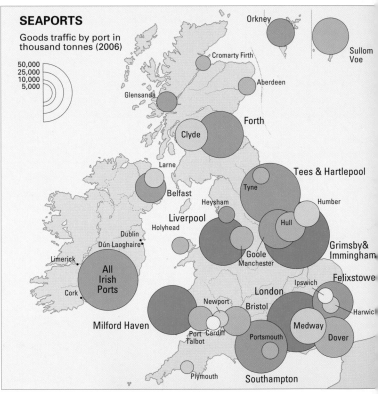

VISITS ABROAD BY U.K. RESIDENTS

Top 10 countries visited (2006)

Number of U.K. visitors (millions)

Countries: Spain, France, Ireland, U.S.A., Greece, Italy, Germany, Netherlands, Belgium, Portugal

Total visits by area in thousands (2006)

North America	4,702
Europe	55,170
Rest of World	9,664
Total	69,536

FOREIGN VISITORS TO THE U.K.

Number of visits (millions)

Nature of visit
- Business
- Leisure

Country of origin
- North America
- European Union
- Other

Years: 1970, 1980, 1990, 2000, 2006

▲ **Eurostar at St. Pancras International.** This newly restored station is the London terminus of the high-speed rail link to Europe, High Speed 1.

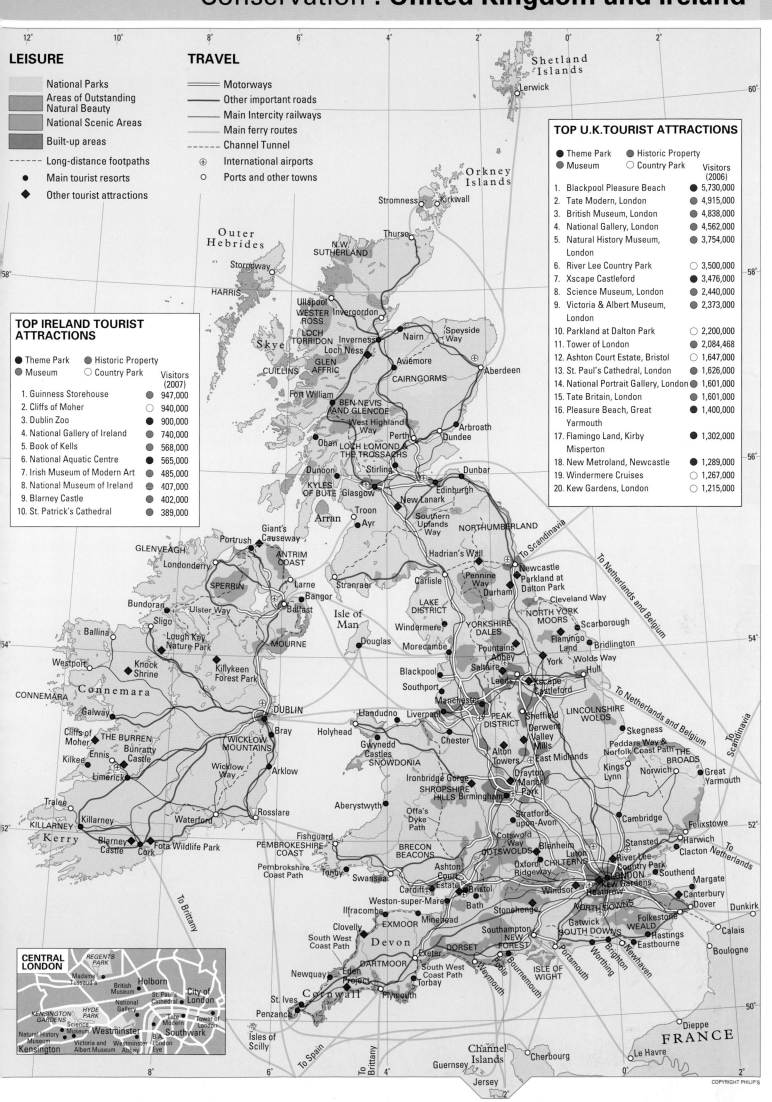

LEISURE

- National Parks
- Areas of Outstanding Natural Beauty
- National Scenic Areas
- Built-up areas
- Long-distance footpaths
- ● Main tourist resorts
- ◆ Other tourist attractions

TRAVEL

- Motorways
- Other important roads
- Main Intercity railways
- Main ferry routes
- Channel Tunnel
- ⊕ International airports
- ○ Ports and other towns

TOP U.K. TOURIST ATTRACTIONS

- ● Theme Park
- ● Museum
- ● Historic Property
- ○ Country Park

		Visitors (2006)
1.	Blackpool Pleasure Beach ●	5,730,000
2.	Tate Modern, London ●	4,915,000
3.	British Museum, London ●	4,838,000
4.	National Gallery, London ●	4,562,000
5.	Natural History Museum, London ●	3,754,000
6.	River Lee Country Park ○	3,500,000
7.	Xscape Castleford ●	3,476,000
8.	Science Museum, London ●	2,440,000
9.	Victoria & Albert Museum, London ●	2,373,000
10.	Parkland at Dalton Park ○	2,200,000
11.	Tower of London ●	2,084,468
12.	Ashton Court Estate, Bristol ○	1,647,000
13.	St. Paul's Cathedral, London ●	1,626,000
14.	National Portrait Gallery, London ●	1,601,000
15.	Tate Britain, London ●	1,601,000
16.	Pleasure Beach, Great Yarmouth ●	1,400,000
17.	Flamingo Land, Kirby Misperton ●	1,302,000
18.	New Metroland, Newcastle ●	1,289,000
19.	Windermere Cruises ○	1,267,000
20.	Kew Gardens, London ○	1,215,000

TOP IRELAND TOURIST ATTRACTIONS

- ● Theme Park
- ● Museum
- ● Historic Property
- ○ Country Park

		Visitors (2007)
1.	Guinness Storehouse ●	947,000
2.	Cliffs of Moher ○	940,000
3.	Dublin Zoo ●	900,000
4.	National Gallery of Ireland ●	740,000
5.	Book of Kells ●	568,000
6.	National Aquatic Centre ●	565,000
7.	Irish Museum of Modern Art ●	485,000
8.	National Museum of Ireland ●	407,000
9.	Blarney Castle ●	402,000
10.	St. Patrick's Cathedral ●	389,000

CENTRAL LONDON

COPYRIGHT PHILIP'S

▲ Oblique satellite image of Europe and North Africa

This image stretches from the white icy landscape of Greenland in the top left-hand side of the image, down to the River Nile and its delta in Egypt in the bottom right-hand corner, and covers all of Europe and the Mediterranean Sea. You can see the difference between the light brown of the more arid land in northern Africa and the more fertile darker and greener land in Europe.

▶ Iceland

This winter image, captured in January, shows Iceland cloaked in snow, covering its four permanent ice caps. The island sits astride the fault line between the North American and Eurasian tectonic plates *(see page 78)*. These are moving away from each other, resulting in a high level of volcanic activity, with much of the land covered in lava flows.

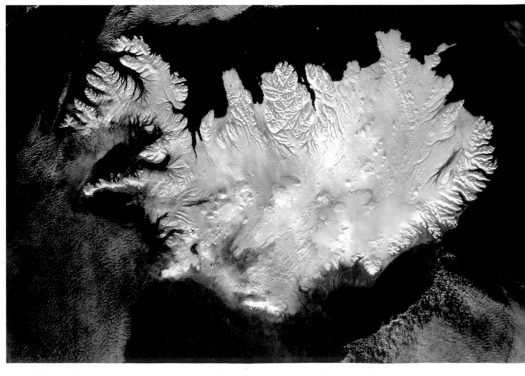

▼ Copenhagen, Denmark

The city, which is the capital of Denmark, faces the town of Malmö in southern Sweden across a narrow strait of water called the Øresund. On the far right of the image is a white linear feature in the sea. This is part of the combined road and railway tunnel and bridge which now links Denmark to Sweden. As a result of this, many people in southern Sweden are nearer to Copenhagen than their own capital city, Stockholm. Many Danes now live in southern Sweden and commute to work in Denmark, creating a new economic region with Copenhagen at its centre.

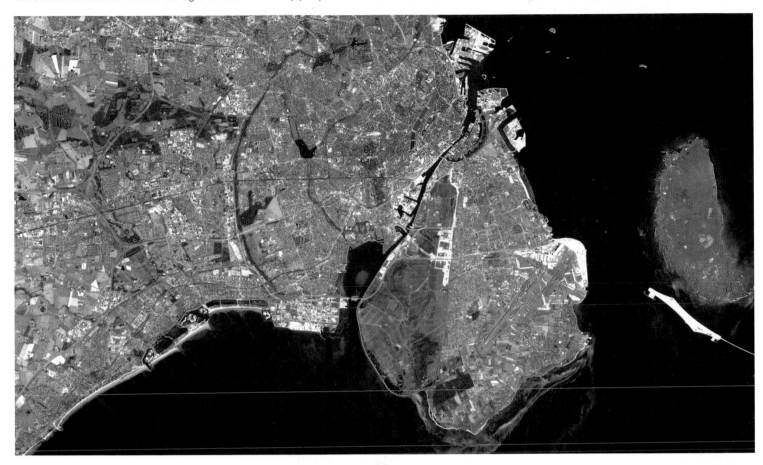

▲ Venice, Italy

The city was built on over 100 small islands in a shallow lagoon as a defensive measure. This image shows the largest island, on which the main part of the city is built. There are no roads so everything is moved by boat and you can see the wakes made by some of the larger boats. The sinuous Grand Canal connects the train station in the top left of the image to St. Mark's Square, on the southern side, with a network of smaller canals on either side.

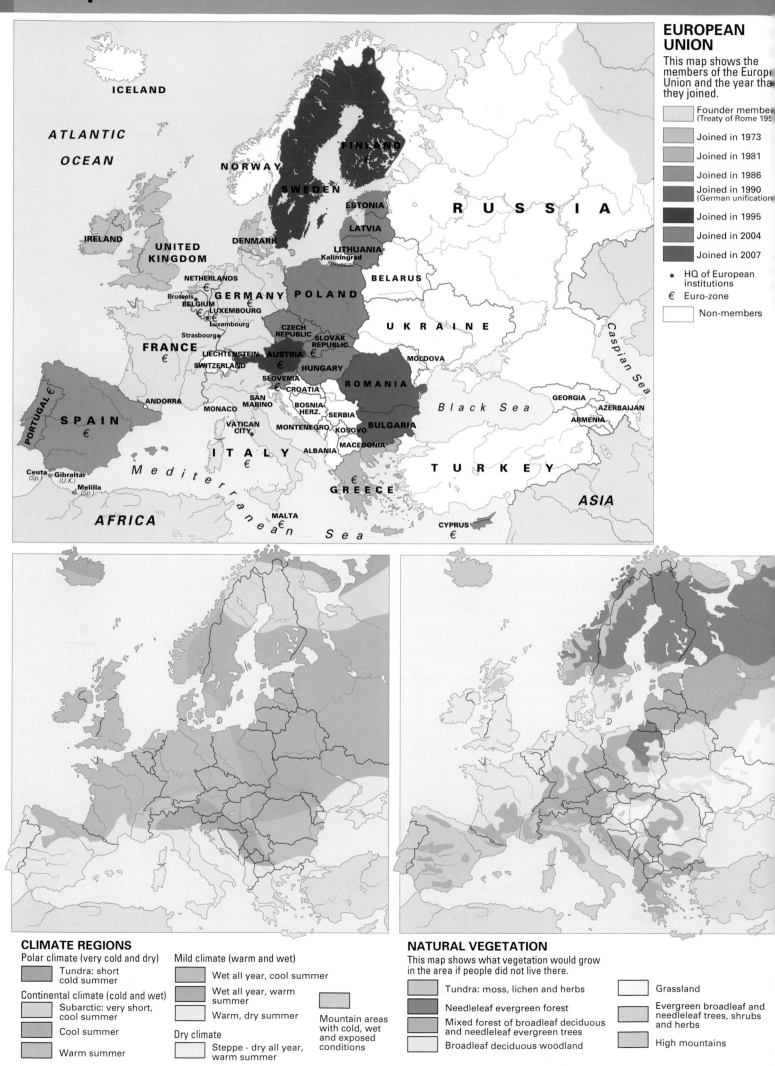

EUROPEAN UNION

This map shows the members of the European Union and the year that they joined.

- Founder member (Treaty of Rome 195...)
- Joined in 1973
- Joined in 1981
- Joined in 1986
- Joined in 1990 (German unification)
- Joined in 1995
- Joined in 2004
- Joined in 2007
- HQ of European institutions
- € Euro-zone
- Non-members

CLIMATE REGIONS

Polar climate (very cold and dry)
- Tundra: short cold summer

Continental climate (cold and wet)
- Subarctic: very short, cool summer
- Cool summer
- Warm summer

Mild climate (warm and wet)
- Wet all year, cool summer
- Wet all year, warm summer
- Warm, dry summer

Dry climate
- Steppe - dry all year, warm summer
- Mountain areas with cold, wet and exposed conditions

NATURAL VEGETATION

This map shows what vegetation would grow in the area if people did not live there.

- Tundra: moss, lichen and herbs
- Needleleaf evergreen forest
- Mixed forest of broadleaf deciduous and needleleaf evergreen trees
- Broadleaf deciduous woodland
- Grassland
- Evergreen broadleaf and needleleaf trees, shrubs and herbs
- High mountains

COPYRIGHT PHILIP'S

POPULATION DENSITY

The number of people per square kilometre

- Over 200
- 100 – 200
- 50 – 100
- 10 – 50
- 1 – 10
- Under 1

Population of major cities

- ● Over 10,000,000
- ■ 5,000,000 – 10,000,000
- ● 2,500,000 – 5,000,000
- ● 1,000,000 – 2,500,000

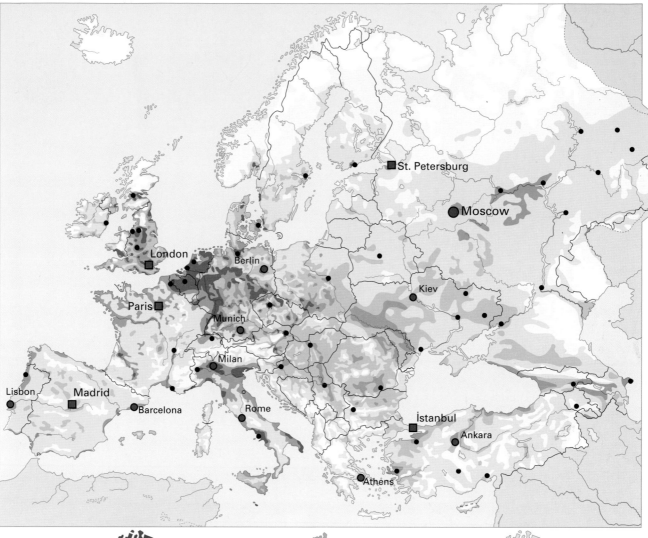

St. Petersburg
Moscow
London
Berlin
Kiev
Paris
Munich
Milan
Lisbon
Madrid
Barcelona
Rome
İstanbul
Ankara
Athens

WEALTH

The value of total production divided by population (2007)

- Over $40,000 per person
- $35,000 – 40,000 per person
- $30,000 – 35,000 per person
- $20,000 – 30,000 per person
- $10,000 – 20,000 per person
- Under $10,000 per person

Wealthiest countries

Luxembourg $80,800 per person
Norway $55,600 per person
Ireland $45,600 per person

Poorest countries

Montenegro $3,800 per person
Moldova $2,200 per person
Kosovo $1,800 per person

Norwegian Fjords
Saimaa
St. Petersburg
Stockholm
Moscow
Edinburgh
Dublin
Copenhagen
Öland
Amsterdam
London
Berlin
Brussels
Prague
Tatra
Brittany
Paris
Disneyland Paris
Vienna
Budapest
Crimea
Alps
Lourdes
Venice
Adriatic Coast
Pyrenees
Black Sea Coast
Lisbon
Côte d'Azur
Florence
Madrid
Costa Brava
Rome
İstanbul
Algarve
Balearic Islands
Ægean Islands
Costa del Sol
Costa Blanca
Ionian Islands
Athens
Rhodes
Crete
Cyprus

TOURISM

Tourism receipts as a percentage of Gross National Income (2005)

- Over 10% of income from tourism
- 5 – 10% of income from tourism
- 2.5 – 5% of income from tourism
- 1 – 2.5% of income from tourism
- Under 1% of income from tourism

Tourist destinations

- ■ Cultural & historical centres
- □ Coastal resorts
- □ Ski resorts
- Centres of entertainment
- Places of pilgrimage
- Places of great natural beauty

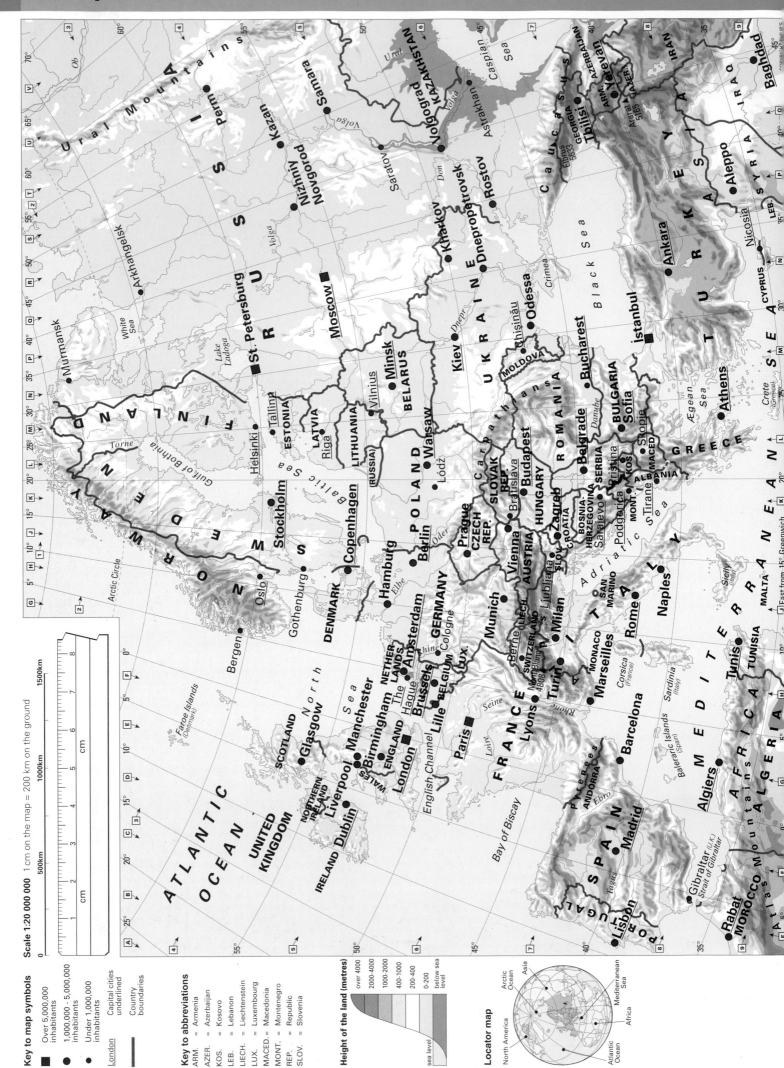

Key to map symbols

■ Over 5,000,000 inhabitants

● 1,000,000 - 5,000,000 inhabitants

• Under 1,000,000 inhabitants

London Capital cities underlined

——— Country boundaries

Key to abbreviations

ARM. = Armenia
AZER. = Azerbaijan
KOS. = Kosovo
LEB. = Lebanon
LIECH. = Liechtenstein
LUX. = Luxembourg
MACED. = Macedonia
MONT. = Montenegro
REP. = Republic
SLOV. = Slovenia

Height of the land (metres)

over 4000
2000-4000
1000-2000
400-1000
200-400
0-200
sea level
below sea level

Locator map

Scale 1:20 000 000   1 cm on the map = 200 km on the ground

0   500km   1000km   1500km

1 cm on the map = 200 km on the ground

Northern Europe

ARCTIC OCEAN

North Cape

Hammerfest
Vardø
Vadsø
Kirkenes
Tromsø
Murmansk

Barents Sea

Vesterålen

Lofoten Islands

Narvik
Kebnekaise ▲ 2123
Kiruna
Gällivare

Lake Inari

Lake Imandra

Kola Peninsula

Kandalaksha

Bodø

Arctic Circle

ATLANTIC OCEAN

Rovaniemi
Kemijärvi

L a p l a n d

Kristiansund

Trondheim

Ålesund

Galdhøpiggen ▲ 2469
Jotunheimen

Storsjön

Östersund

Kemi
Kemi

Luleå

Skellefteå

Oulu

Belomorsk

White Sea

Arkhangelsk

Onega

65°

N o r r l a n d

Ume

Umeå

Kajaani

Lake Oulu

K a r e l i a

Bergen

Hardanger Fjord

Sogne Fjord

Lillehammer

Glåma

Mjøsa Lake

Vaasa
Kuopio
Joensuu

FINLAND

Jyväskylä

Lake Onega

Petrozavodsk

Haugesund
Drammen
Oslo

Stavanger
Fredrikstad

Kristiansand

S v e a l a n d

Gävle

Gulf of Bothnia

Pori
Tampere
Lahti

Lake Saimaa

Lake Ladoga

Vyborg

60°

Västerås

Uppsala

Åland Islands

Turku

Helsinki

Kotka

St. Petersburg

Cherepovets

Örebro
Lake Väner
Stockholm

Göta Canal
Norrköping
Lake Vätter
Linköping

Hiiumaa

Saaremaa

Tallinn

ESTONIA

Lake Chudskoye

Novgorod

Rybinsk Reservoir

Skagerrak
Skagen
Gothenburg
Borås
Jönköping
Götaland

Gulf of Riga

Pskov

RUSSIA

Tver

Aalborg
DENMARK
Jutland
Aarhus
Kattegat

Gotland

Öland

Riga
Liepāja

LATVIA

West Dvina

Moscow

55°
Copenhagen
Helsingborg
Esbjerg
Odense
Sjaelland
Malmö

Bornholm

Baltic Sea

Klaipėda

LITHUANIA
Kaunas

Vitebsk

Smolensk
Kaluga

Kiel Canal
Kiel

Rostock

Kaliningrad
(RUSSIA)
Vilnius

Minsk
Mogilev

Bryansk

NETH.

Hamburg
Bremen

Szczecin

Gdańsk

Vistula

Neman

BELARUS

Gomel

Hanover
Berlin

Oder

Bydgoszcz

Białystok

Pripet

Dnepr

GERMANY

Dortmund
Poznań
POLAND

Leipzig

Cologne
Bonn
Dresden
Wrocław
Łódź
Warsaw
Brest
Lublin

Chernobyl

Kiev

Frankfurt

Rhine

CZECH REP.
Prague
Kraków

Bug

UKRAINE

Zhitomir

East from Greenwich

COPYRIGHT PHILIP'S

Scale 1:10 000 000   1 cm on the map = 100 km on the ground

0   100km   200km   300km   400km   500km   600km

cm   cm

Height of the land (metres)

over 4000
2000-4000
1000-2000
400-1000
200-400
0-200
sea level
below sea level

Key to map symbols

■ Over 5,000,000 inhabitants

● 1,000,000 - 5,000,000 inhabitants

• Under 1,000,000 inhabitants

<u>Helsinki</u> Capital cities underlined

— Country boundaries

Locator map

Height of the land (metres)

over 4000
2000-4000
1000-2000
400-1000
200-400
0-200
below sea level
sea level

Key to map symbols

■ Over 5,000,000 inhabitants
● 1,000,000 - 5,000,000 inhabitants
• Under 1,000,000 inhabitants
Paris Capital cities underlined
Country boundaries

Locator map

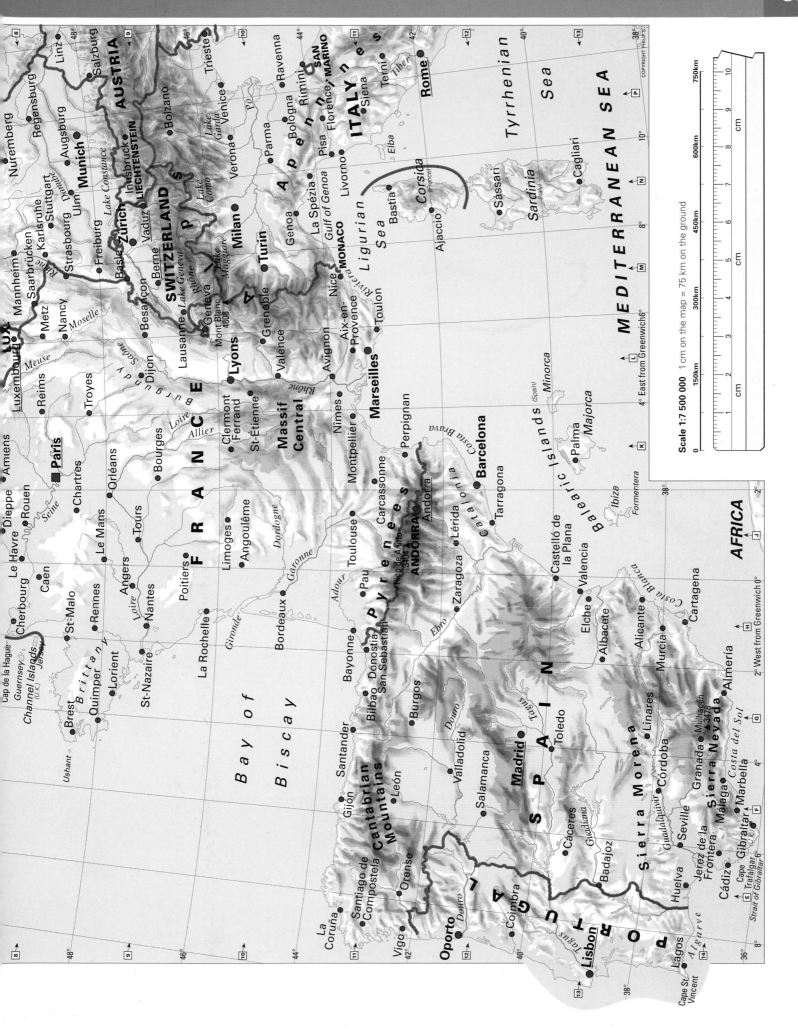

Scale 1:7 500 000 1cm on the map = 75 km on the ground

4° East from Greenwich 6°

2° West from Greenwich 0°

0   150km   300km   450km   600km   750km

cm   1   2   3   4   5   6   7   8   9   10   cm

MEDITERRANEAN SEA

Tyrrhenian Sea

ITALY

Rome

Tiber

Terni

Siena

Florence

Pisa

Livorno

Bologna

Ravenna

Rimini

SAN MARINO

Parma

Verona

Venice

Lake Garda

Lake Como

Bolzano

Trieste

Po

A p e n n i n e s

Genoa

Gulf of Genoa

La Spézia

MONACO

Nice

Riviera

Ligurian Sea

△ Elba

Corsica (France)

Bastia

Ajaccio

Sardinia (Italy)

Sássari

Cagliari

SWITZERLAND

Zurich

Basle

Berne

Lausanne

Lake Geneva

Geneva

Mont Blanc 4808

A l p s

Vaduz

LIECHTENSTEIN

Innsbruck

AUSTRIA

Salzburg

Linz

Munich

Ulm

Augsburg

Regensburg

Nuremberg

Stuttgart

Karlsruhe

Freiburg

Strasbourg

Saarbrücken

Mannheim

Metz

Nancy

Reims

LUX

Luxembourg

Meuse

Moselle

Rhine

Danube

Lake Constance

FRANCE

Paris

Amiens

Dieppe

Le Havre

Rouen

Caen

Chartres

Orléans

Troyes

Dijon

Besançon

B u r g u n d y

Saône

Lyons

Grenoble

Valence

Avignon

Aix-en-Provence

Marseilles

Toulon

Nîmes

Montpellier

Perpignan

St-Étienne

Clermont Ferrand

Massif Central

Bourges

Allier

Loire

Turin

Milan

Lake Maggiore

Rhône

Rhône

Dordogne

Garonne

Limoges

Angoulême

Poitiers

Tours

Angers

Le Mans

Nantes

St-Nazaire

Lorient

Quimper

Brest

Rennes

St-Malo

Cherbourg

Cap de la Hague

Guernsey (U.K.)

Jersey

Channel Islands (U.K.)

Ushant

B r i t t a n y

Seine

Bay

of

Biscay

La Rochelle

Bordeaux

Gironde

Bayonne

Pau

Adour

Toulouse

Carcassonne

P y r e n e e s

Pico de Aneto 3404 △

ANDORRA

Andorra

Catalonia

Barcelona

Costa Brava

Tarragona

Lérida

Zaragoza

Ebro

SPAIN

Donostia/San Sebastián

Bilbao

Santander

Gijón

La Coruña

Santiago de Compostela

Cantabrian Mountains

León

Burgos

Valladolid

Salamanca

Madrid

Toledo

Cáceres

Badajoz

Guadiana

Tagus

Douro

Douro

Orense

Vigo

PORTUGAL

Oporto

Coimbra

Lisbon

Tagus

Lagos

Algarve

Cape St. Vincent

Huelva

Sevilla

Guadalquivir

Córdoba

Jerez de la Frontera

Cádiz

Cape Trafalgar

Gibraltar

Strait of Gibraltar

Marbella

Málaga

Costa del Sol

Granada

Sierra Nevada

Mulhacén 3478

Sierra Morena

Linares

Albacete

Murcia

Cartagena

Almería

Alicante

Elche

Valencia

Castelló de la Plana

Costa Blanca

Balearic Islands (Spain)

Minorca

Majorca

Palma

Ibiza

Formentera

AFRICA

Height of the land (metres)

- over 4000
- 2000-4000
- 1000-2000
- 400-1000
- 200-400
- 0-200
- below sea level

sea level

Key to map symbols

- ■ Over 5,000,000 inhabitants
- ● 1,000,000 - 5,000,000 inhabitants
- • Under 1,000,000 inhabitants
- <u>Sofia</u> Capital cities underlined
- — Country boundaries
- ⁚∴ Historical site
- Seasonal lake

Scale 1:10 000 000   1 cm on the map = 100 km on the ground

0   250km   500km   750km   1000km

cm   cm   cm

Cross-section along latitude 45°N

FRANCE   ITALY   ROMANIA

Bay of Biscay   Massif Central   Mont Blanc 4808 Alps   Po   Adriatic Sea   Dinaric Alps   Sava   Danube   Transylvanian Alps   Danube   Black Sea

Mont Dore 1886   Rhone

45°N   45°N

Locator map

Height of the land (metres)

over 6000
3000 – 6000
2000 – 3000
1000 – 2000
400 – 1000
200 – 400
0 – 200
sea level
below sea
level

Key to map symbols

Over 1,000,000
inhabitants

500,000 – 1,000,000
inhabitants

Under 500,000
inhabitants

Rome Capital cities

Country boundaries

Historical site

Scale 1:5 000 000   1 cm on the map = 50 km on the ground

0   50km   100km   150km   200km   250km   300km

cm

Regions

VALLE
D'AOSTA
ALTO ADIGE
TRENTINO
FRIULI-VENEZIA
GIULA
LOMBARDY
PIEDMONT
VENETO
LIGURIA
EMILIA-
ROMAGNA
TUSCANY
MARCHE
UMBRIA
ABRUZZO
LAZIO
MOLISE
SARDINIA
PUGLIA
CAMPANIA
BASILICATA
CALABRIA
SICILY

Area 301,270 sq km
Population 58,148,000
Capital (population) Rome (2,688,000)

Locator map

COPYRIGHT PHILIP'S

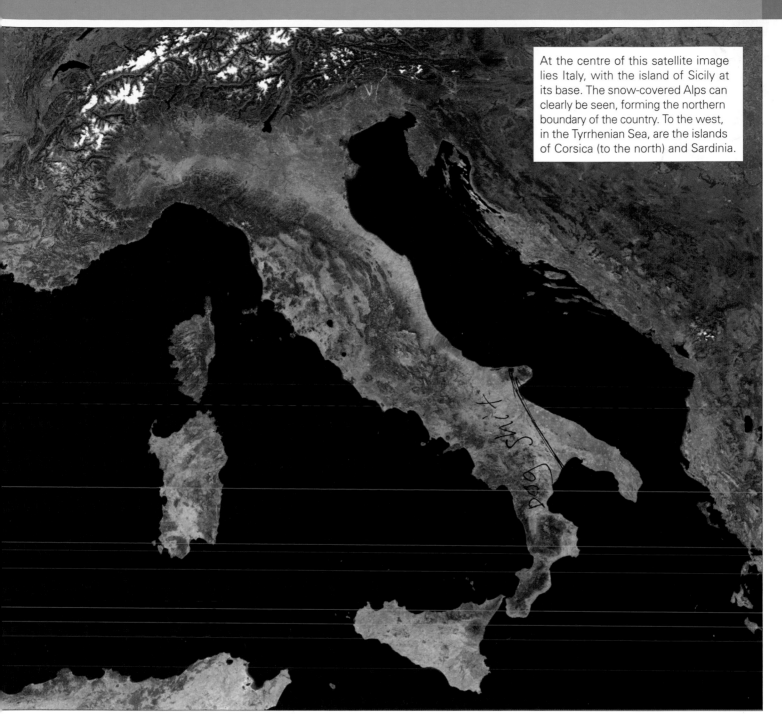

At the centre of this satellite image lies Italy, with the island of Sicily at its base. The snow-covered Alps can clearly be seen, forming the northern boundary of the country. To the west, in the Tyrrhenian Sea, are the islands of Corsica (to the north) and Sardinia.

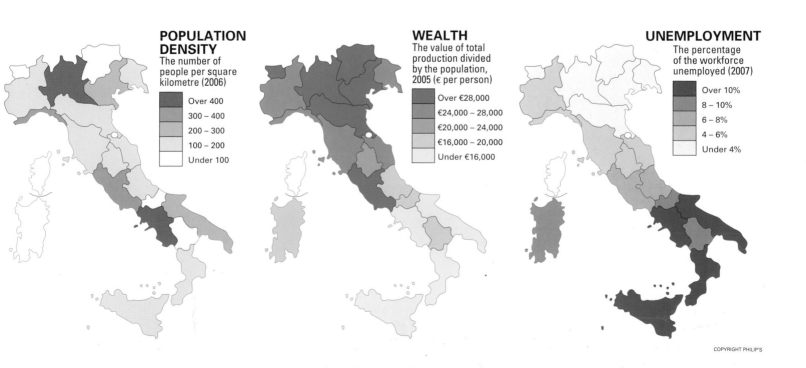

POPULATION DENSITY
The number of people per square kilometre (2006)

- Over 400
- 300 – 400
- 200 – 300
- 100 – 200
- Under 100

WEALTH
The value of total production divided by the population, 2005 (€ per person)

- Over €28,000
- €24,000 – 28,000
- €20,000 – 24,000
- €16,000 – 20,000
- Under €16,000

UNEMPLOYMENT
The percentage of the workforce unemployed (2007)

- Over 10%
- 8 – 10%
- 6 – 8%
- 4 – 6%
- Under 4%

Height of the land (metres)

over 6000
4000-6000
2000-4000
1000-2000
400-1000
200-400
0-200
below sea level

sea level

Key to map symbols

■ Over 5,000,000 inhabitants

● 1,000,000 - 5,000,000 inhabitants

• Under 1,000,000 inhabitants

Kiev Capital cities underlined

─── Country boundaries

Scale 1:20 000 000 1 cm on the map = 200 km on the ground

Locator map

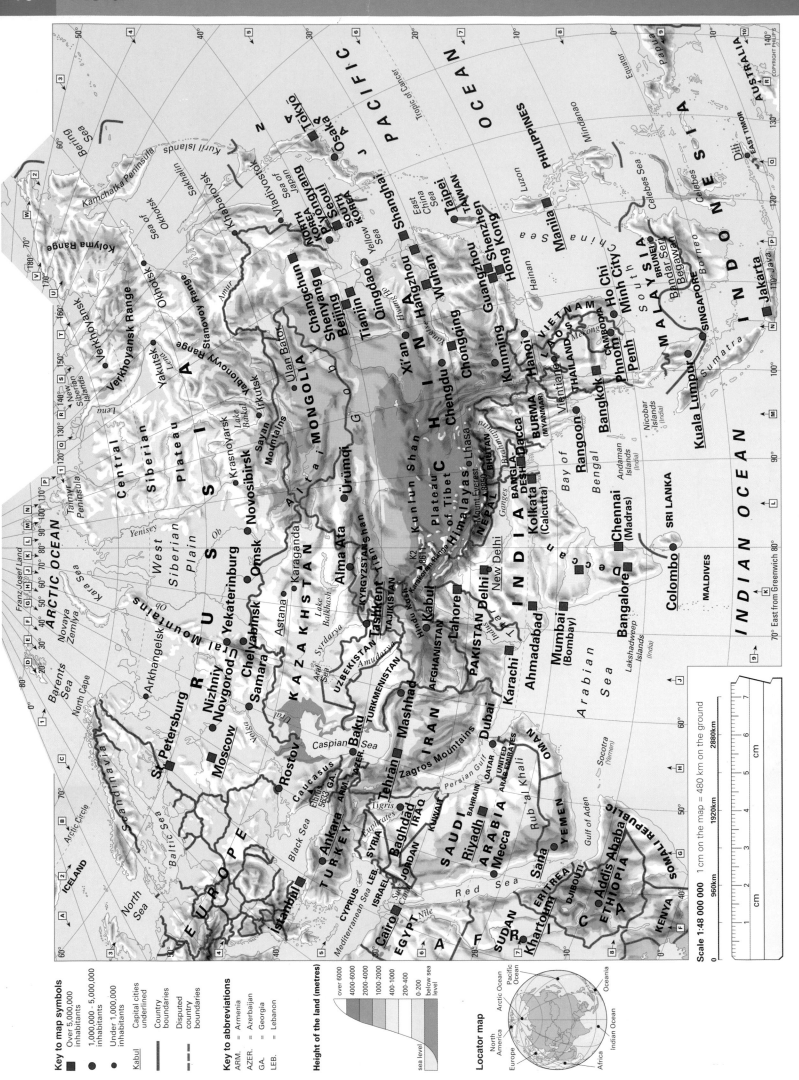

Key to map symbols

■ Over 5,000,000 inhabitants

● 1,000,000 – 5,000,000 inhabitants

• Under 1,000,000 inhabitants

Kabul Capital cities underlined

— Country boundaries

— Disputed country boundaries

Key to abbreviations

ARM. = Armenia
AZER. = Azerbaijan
GA. = Georgia
LEB. = Lebanon

Height of the land (metres)

over 6000
4000–6000
2000–4000
1000–2000
400–1000
200–400
0–200
below sea level

sea level

Locator map

Arctic Ocean
North America
Europe
Asia
Africa
Pacific Ocean
Indian Ocean
Oceania

Scale 1:48 000 000

1 cm on the map = 480 km on the ground

0   960km   1920km   2880km

0   1   2   3   4   5   6   7   cm

COPYRIGHT PHILIP'S

INDUSTRIAL DEVELOPMENT

- Core industrial regions
- ● Major centres for industry
- • Centres for iron and steel, and chemicals
- Rapidly developing coastal regions
- ■ Special Economic Zones
- ▼ Special Administrative Regions
- Outer industrial regions
- Outer industrial regions with traditional heavy industry
- Remote undeveloped regions
- → Direction of future growth
- — Important rail links

Area 9,596,960 sq km
Population 1,321,851,888
Capital (population) Beijing (10,849,000)

Direction of foreign investment
← from Hong Kong   ← from Taiwan
← from Japan   ← from South Korea

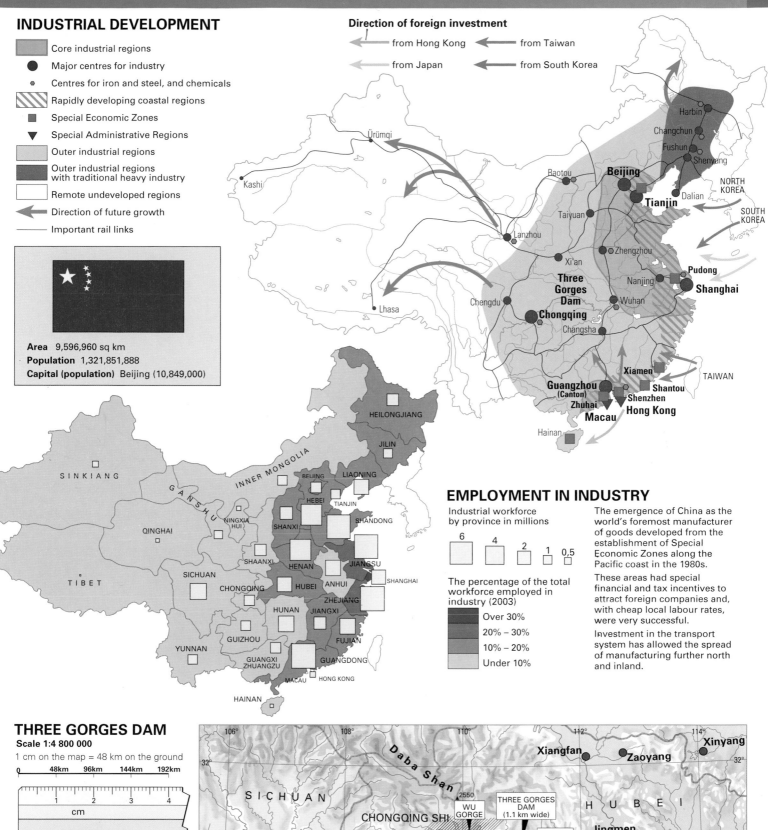

EMPLOYMENT IN INDUSTRY

Industrial workforce by province in millions

6   4   2   1   0.5

The percentage of the total workforce employed in industry (2003)

- Over 30%
- 20% – 30%
- 10% – 20%
- Under 10%

The emergence of China as the world's foremost manufacturer of goods developed from the establishment of Special Economic Zones along the Pacific coast in the 1980s.

These areas had special financial and tax incentives to attract foreign companies and, with cheap local labour rates, were very successful.

Investment in the transport system has allowed the spread of manufacturing further north and inland.

THREE GORGES DAM

Scale 1:4 800 000

1 cm on the map = 48 km on the ground

0   48km   96km   144km   192km

cm

Height of the land (metres)

- over 2000
- 1500 – 2000
- 1000 – 1500
- 400 – 1000
- 200 – 400
- 0 – 200
- below sea level

- ■ Over 5,000,000 inhabitants
- ● 1,000,000 – 5,000,000 inhabitants
- • Under 1,000,000 inhabitants

- Reservoir over 600 m long
- Surface area over 1000 km²
- Over 630 km² flooded
- 1,200,000 people had to relocate

COPYRIGHT PHILIP'S

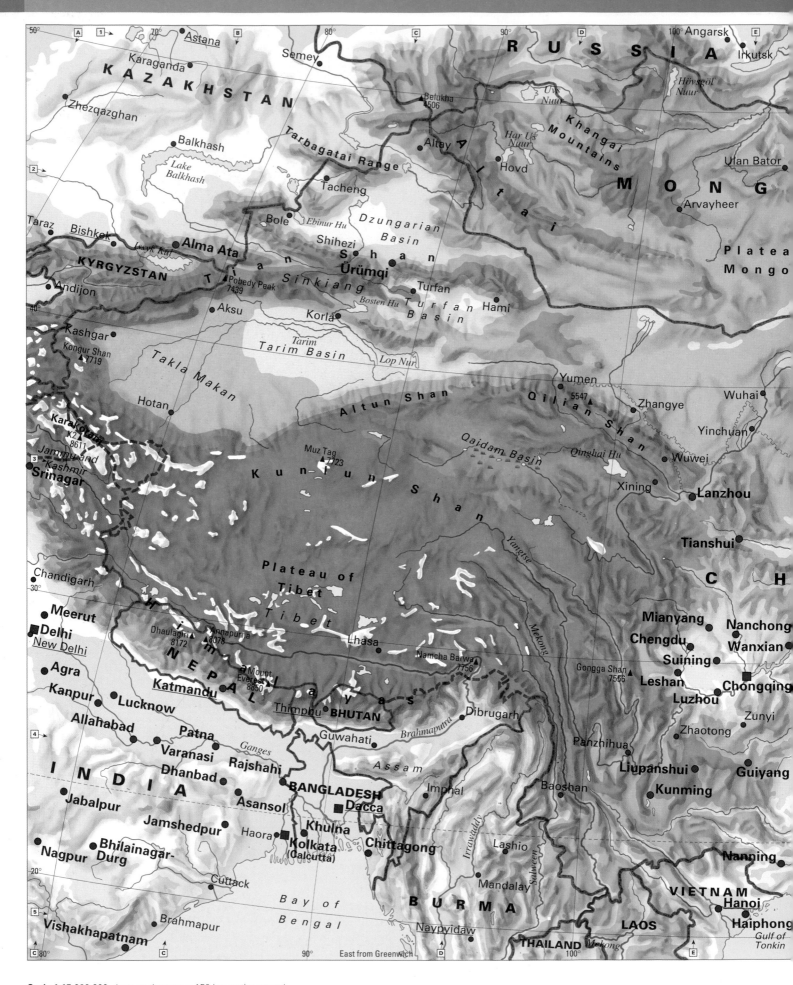

Scale 1:15 000 000   1 cm on the map = 150 km on the ground

0   300km   600km   900km   1200km   1500km

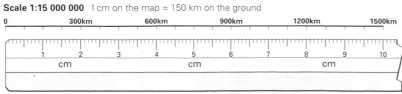

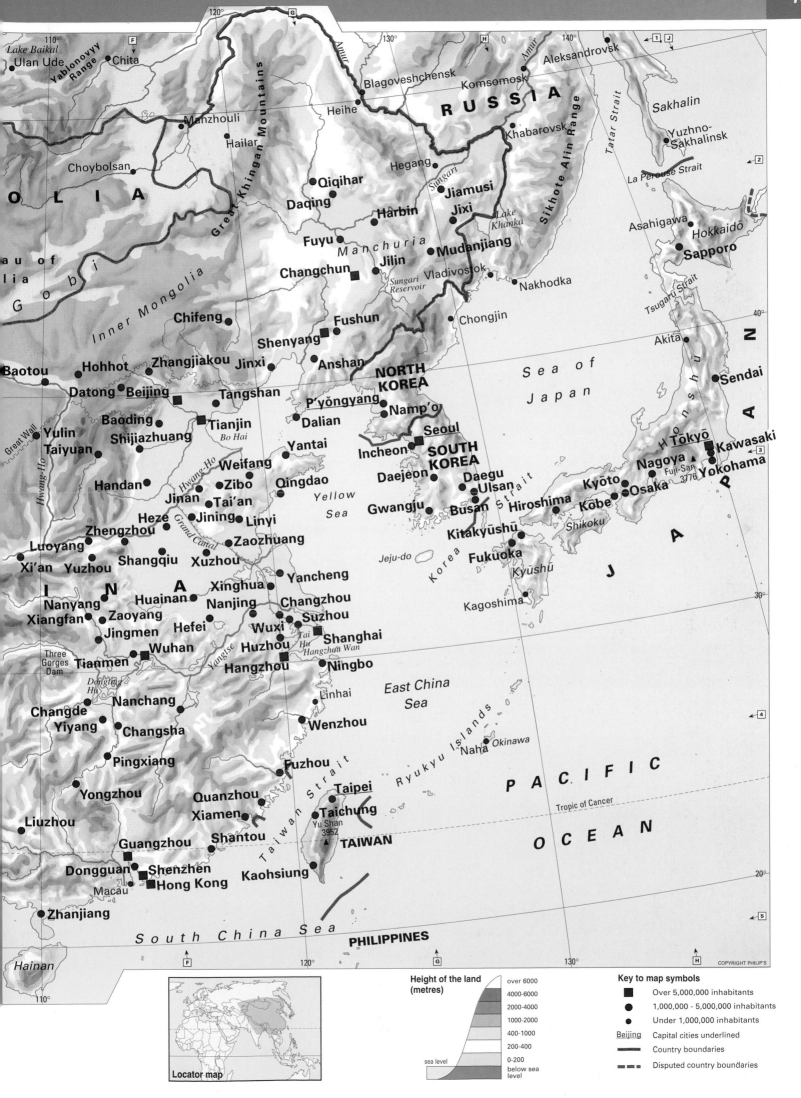

Height of the land (metres)

over 6000
4000-6000
2000-4000
1000-2000
400-1000
200-400
0-200
sea level
below sea level

Key to map symbols

■ Over 5,000,000 inhabitants

● 1,000,000 - 5,000,000 inhabitants

• Under 1,000,000 inhabitants

Beijing Capital cities underlined

── Country boundaries

─ ─ Disputed country boundaries

Locator map

COPYRIGHT PHILIP'S

Scale 1:7 500 000   1 cm on the map = 75 km on the ground

0   75km   150km   225km   300km   375km   450km

Height of the land (metres)

over 4000
2000–4000
1000–2000
400–1000
200–400
0–200
sea level
below sea level

Key to map symbols

■ Over 5,000,000 inhabitants

● 1,000,000 – 5,000,000 inhabitants

• Under 1,000,000 inhabitants

Tōkyō Capital cities underlined

━━ Country boundaries

Locator map

COPYRIGHT PHILIP'S

VOLCANOES AND EARTHQUAKES

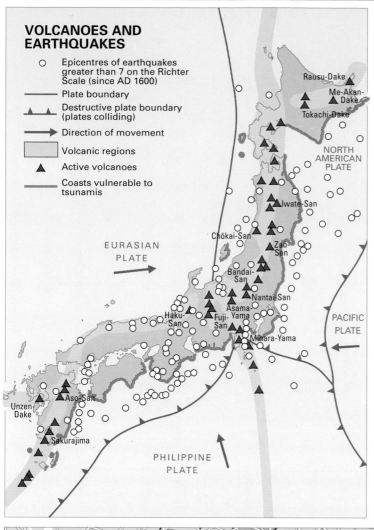

- ○ Epicentres of earthquakes greater than 7 on the Richter Scale (since AD 1600)
- — Plate boundary
- ▲ Destructive plate boundary (plates colliding)
- → Direction of movement
- ▨ Volcanic regions
- ▲ Active volcanoes
- — Coasts vulnerable to tsunamis

Rausu-Dake
Me-Akan-Dake
Tokachi-Dake

NORTH AMERICAN PLATE

Iwate-San
Chōkai-San
Zaō-San
Bandai-San
Nantai-San
Asama-Yama
Haku-San
Fuji-San
Mihara-Yama

EURASIAN PLATE

PACIFIC PLATE

Aso-San
Unzen-Dake
Sakurajima

PHILIPPINE PLATE

POPULATION

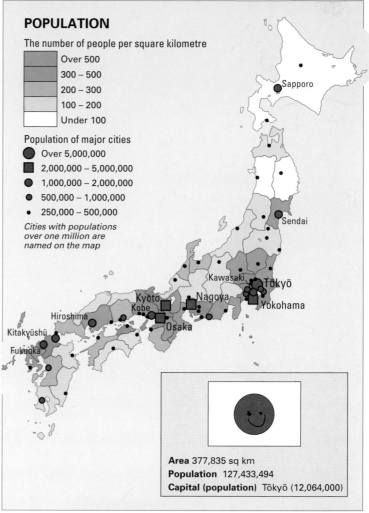

The number of people per square kilometre
- Over 500
- 300 – 500
- 200 – 300
- 100 – 200
- Under 100

Population of major cities
- ● Over 5,000,000
- ■ 2,000,000 – 5,000,000
- ● 1,000,000 – 2,000,000
- ● 500,000 – 1,000,000
- • 250,000 – 500,000

Cities with populations over one million are named on the map

Sapporo
Sendai
Kawasaki Tōkyō
Kyōto Nagoya Yokohama
Kobe
Hiroshima Osaka
Kitakyūshū
Fukuoka

Area 377,835 sq km
Population 127,433,494
Capital (population) Tōkyō (12,064,000)

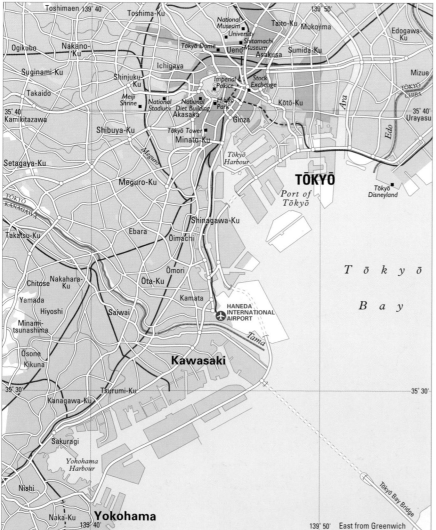

Toshimaen
Toshima-Ku
Taito-Ku Mukōjima
National Museum
University Shitamachi Museum
Tōkyō Dome Ueno Asakusa
Ogikubo Nakano-Ku Edogawa-Ku
Suginami-Ku Ichigaya Sumida-Ku
Takaido Shinjuku-Ku Mizue
Meiji Shrine Imperial Palace Stock Exchange
Kamikitazawa National Stadium National Diet Building Hibiya Park Kōtō-Ku Urayasu
Shibuya-Ku Akasaka Ginza
Setagaya-Ku Tōkyō Tower
Meguro-Ku Minato-Ku
Tōkyō Harbour
Tōkyō Tōkyō Disneyland
Meguro-Ku **TŌKYŌ**
Port of Tōkyō
Shinagawa-Ku
Ebara
Ōimachi
Chitose Nakahara-Ku Ōmori
Yamada Kamata
Hiyoshi Saiwai
Minami-tsunashima HANEDA INTERNATIONAL AIRPORT
Ōsone
Kikuna **Kawasaki** *Tōkyō Bay*
Tsurumi-Ku
Kanagawa-Ku
Sakuragi
Yokohama Harbour Tōkyō Bay Bridge
Nishi Naka-Ku **Yokohama** East from Greenwich

◄▲ Comparing the map of Tōkyō on the left with this satellite image helps to identify specific areas and features.

TŌKYŌ

Scale 1:250 000

1 cm on the map = 2.5 km on the ground

0 2km 4km 6km 8km 10km

- ▨ Central business district
- ▨ Urban area
- ▨ Park and open space
- ═ Motorway
- ═ Other road
- — Railway
- ✈ Airport
- ■ Place of interest
- ⋯ Prefectural boundary

COPYRIGHT PHILIP'S

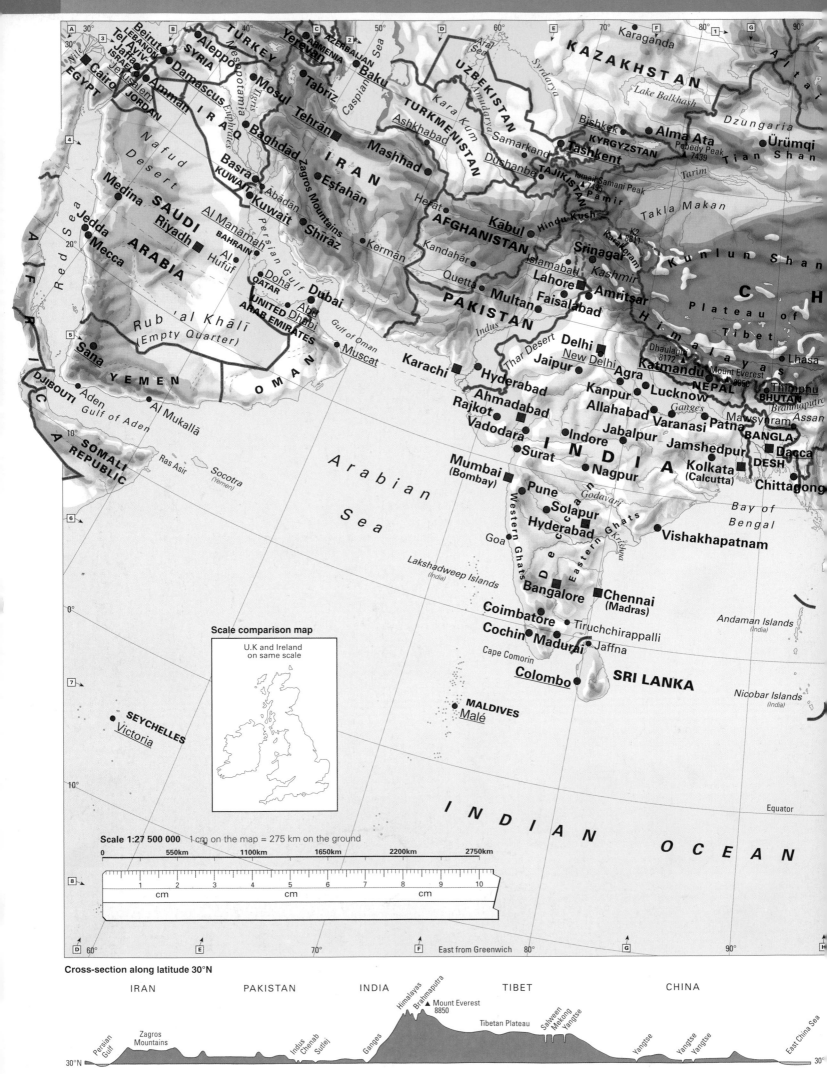

Scale comparison map

U.K and Ireland
on same scale

SEYCHELLES
Victoria

Scale 1:27 500 000   1 cm on the map = 275 km on the ground

| 0 | 550km | 1100km | 1650km | 2200km | 2750km |

Cross-section along latitude 30°N

IRAN   PAKISTAN   INDIA   TIBET   CHINA

Height of the land (metres)

over 6000	
4000-6000	
2000-4000	
1000-2000	
400-1000	
200-400	
0-200	
sea level	
below sea level	

Locator map

Key to map symbols

■ Over 5,000,000 inhabitants

● 1,000,000 – 5,000,000 inhabitants

• Under 1,000,000 inhabitants

Beijing   Capital cities underlined

——   Country boundaries

- - -   Disputed country boundaries

  Seasonal lakes

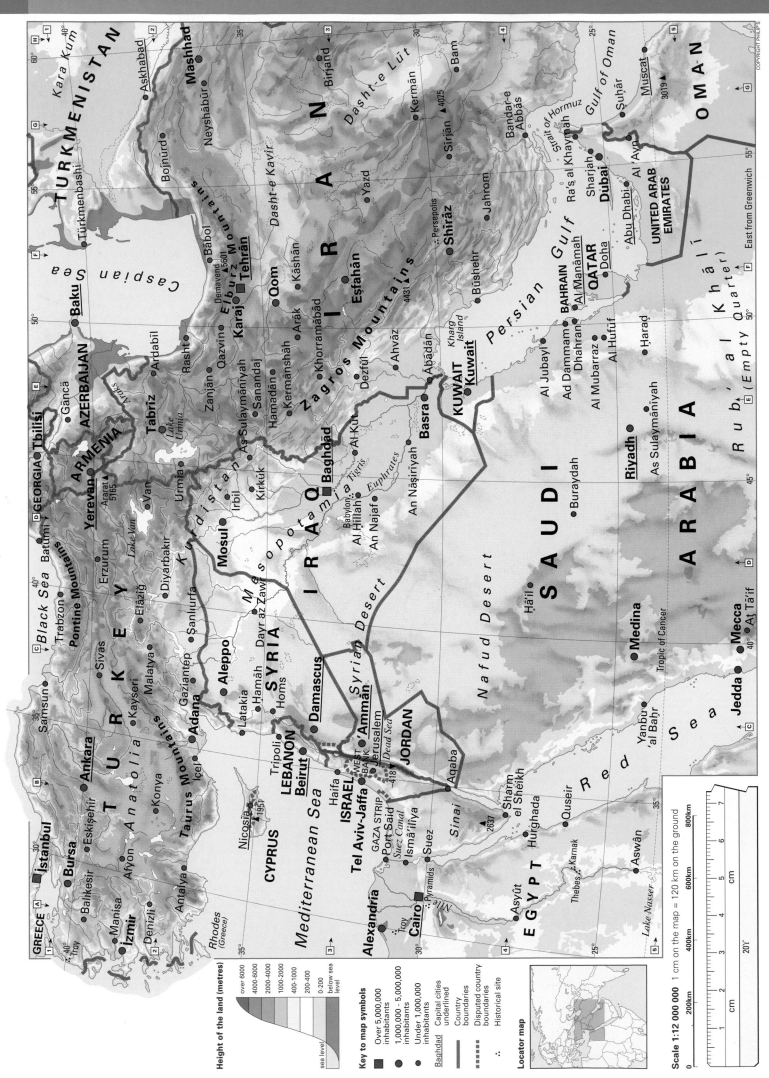

Height of the land (metres)

over 6000
4000-6000
2000-4000
1000-2000
400-1000
200-400
0-200
below sea level

sea level

Key to map symbols

■ Over 5,000,000 inhabitants
● 1,000,000 - 5,000,000 inhabitants
• Under 1,000,000 inhabitants

Baghdad Capital cities underlined

—— Country boundaries

‐‐‐ Disputed country boundaries

.·. Historical site

Locator map

Scale 1:12 000 000 1 cm on the map = 120 km on the ground

0 200km 400km 600km 800km

COPYRIGHT PHILIP'S

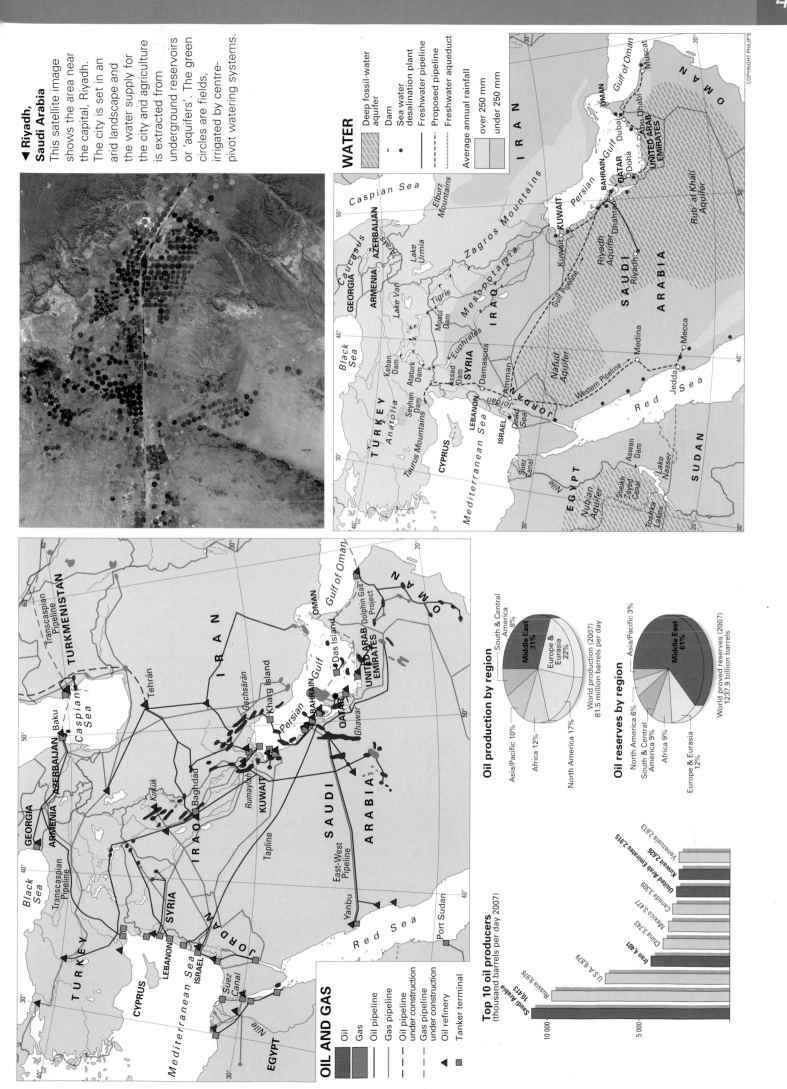

▲ Riyadh, Saudi Arabia

This satellite image shows the area near the capital, Riyadh. The city is set in an arid landscape and the water supply for the city and agriculture is extracted from underground reservoirs or 'aquifers'. The green circles are fields, irrigated by centre-pivot watering systems.

WATER

Deep fossil-water aquifer
Dam
Sea water desalination plant
Freshwater pipeline
Proposed pipeline
Freshwater aqueduct

Average annual rainfall
over 250 mm
under 250 mm

COPYRIGHT PHILIP'S

OIL AND GAS

Oil
Gas
Oil pipeline
Gas pipeline
Oil pipeline under construction
Gas pipeline under construction
Oil refinery
Tanker terminal

Oil production by region

South & Central America 8%
Middle East 31%
Europe & Eurasia 22%
North America 17%
Africa 12%
Asia/Pacific 10%

World production (2007)
81.5 million barrels per day

Oil reserves by region

North America 6%
South & Central America 3%
Africa 9%
Europe & Eurasia 12%
Middle East 61%
Asia/Pacific 3%

World proved reserves (2007)
1237.9 billion barrels

Top 10 oil producers
(thousand barrels per day 2007)

Saudi Arabia 10,413
Russia 9,978
U.S.A. 6,879
Iran 4,401
China 3,743
Mexico 3,477
Canada 3,309
United Arab Emirates 2,915
Kuwait 2,626
Venezuela 2,613

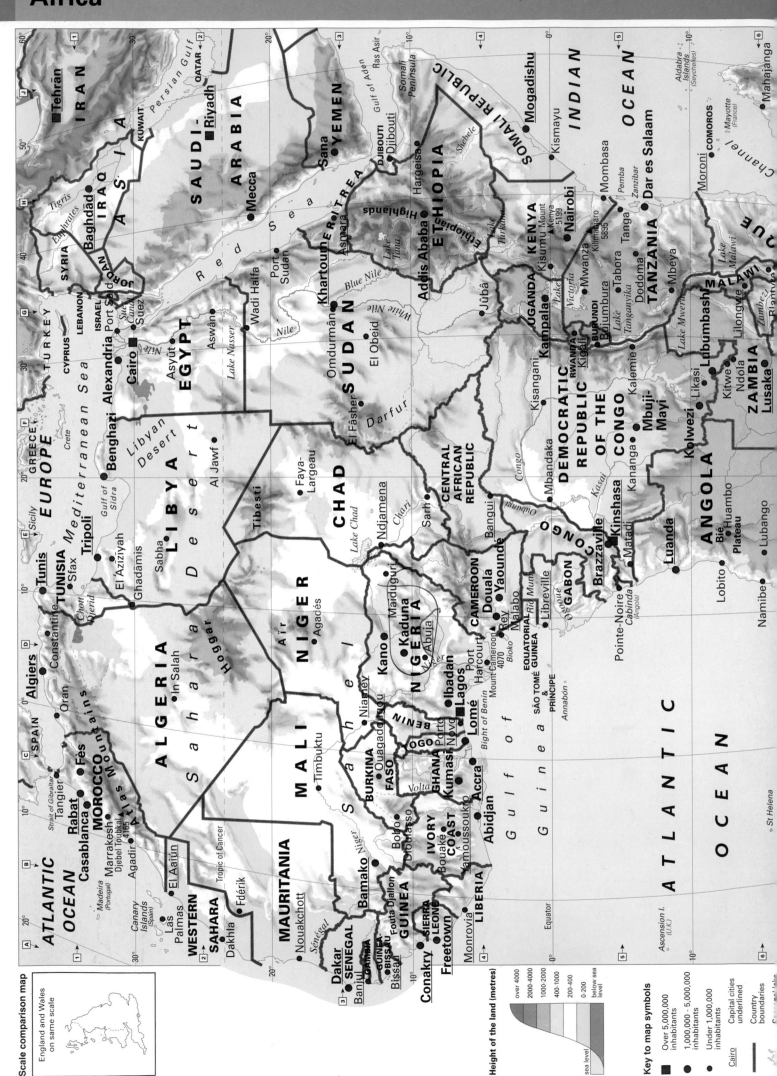

Scale comparison map

England and Wales
on same scale

Height of the land (metres)

over 4000
2000-4000
1000-2000
400-1000
200-400
0-200
below sea
level

sea level

Key to map symbols

■ Over 5,000,000
inhabitants

● 1,000,000 - 5,000,000
inhabitants

• Under 1,000,000
inhabitants

Cairo Capital cities
underlined

Country
boundaries

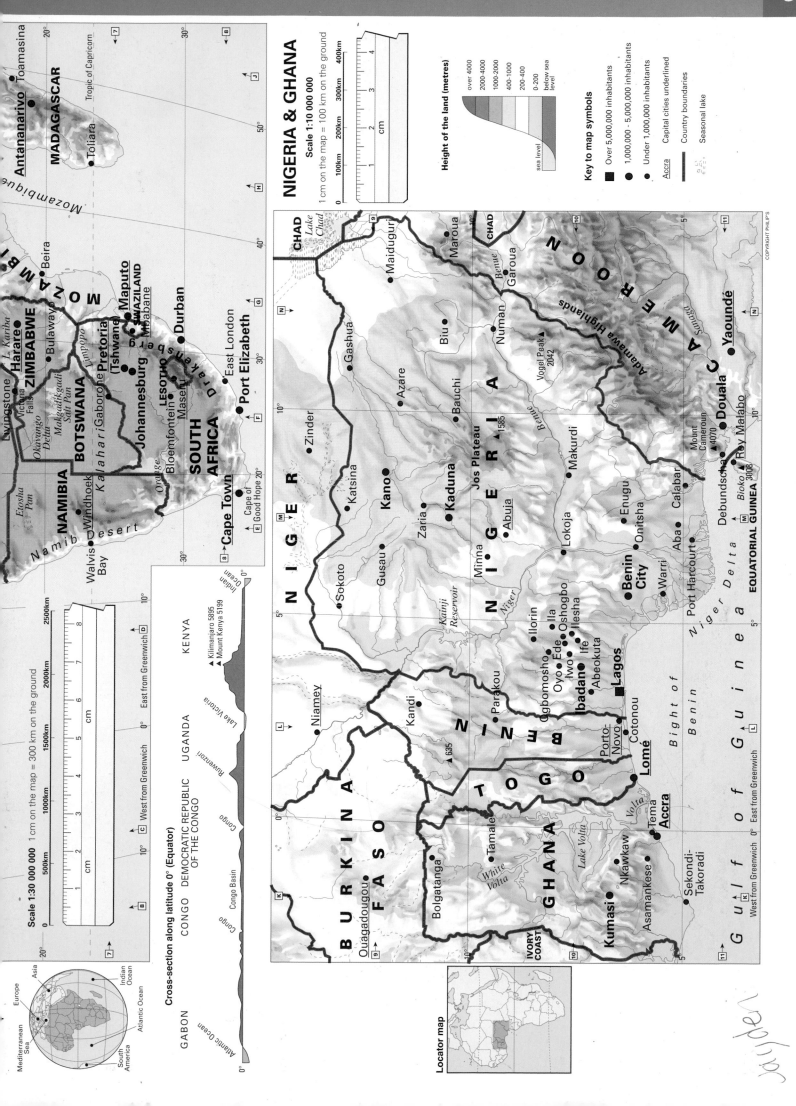

Scale 1:5 000 000 1 cm on the map = 50 km on the ground

0 50km 100km 150km 200km 250km 300km 350km 400km

1 2 3 4 5 6 7 8
cm cm

SUDAN

Elemi Triangle

ETHIOPIA

Mandera

▲ Kinyeti 3187

Chew Bahir (Lake Stefanie)

Lokitaung

375

Moyale

Sololo

El Wak

Kakuma

Lake Turkana

North Horr

Kitgum

Lodwar

Kargi

UGANDA

Moroto 3084

Lockichar

South Horr

Marsabit

Wajir

SOMALI REPUBLIC

Lira

Turkwel

Ndoto Mountains

Lagh Bor

Soroti

Lake Kyoga

Kapenguria
Mount Elgon

Maralal

Merti

Mbale

Kitale

Mado Gashi

Lagh Dera

Tororo
Bungoma

Tambach
Kabarnet

Isiolo

Jinja
Mukono

Busia
Kakamega

Eldoret

Nanyuki

Meru

Liboi

Nyahururu

Kisumu

Winam Gulf

Molo

Nakuru

Aberdare Range
Nyeri

Mount Kenya 5199

Garissa

Tana

Kericho

Gilgil

Homa Bay

Naivasha

Embu

Kisii

Lake Naivasha

Lake

Bomet

Mwingi

Migori

Kilgoris

Thua

Hola

Victoria

Narok

Kiambu

Thika

Kitui

Tarime

Musoma

1134

Magadi

Nairobi

Machakos

Ukerewe Island

Kajiado

Garsen

Lamu

Lake Natron

Kibwezi

Mwanza

Serengeti Plain

Ungwana Bay

TANZANIA

Tsavo

Galana

Malindi

Ngorongoro Crater 3188 ▲

Kilimanjaro 5895 ▲

Voi

Kilifi

Arusha 4565

Meru

Moshi

INDIAN

Lake Manyara

Mombasa
Kilindini

Kwale

OCEAN

Masai Steppe

Pare Mountains

Pemba Island
Wete

Korogwe East from Greenwich 37°30' **Tanga** 40°

COPYRIGHT PHILIP'S

Height of the land (metres)

over 4000
2000-4000
1000-2000
400-1000
200-400
0-200
below sea level
sea level

Key to map symbols

■ 1,000,000 - 5,000,000 inhabitants
● Under 1,000,000 inhabitants
Nairobi Capital cities underlined
—— Country boundaries
----- Seasonal rivers
▨ Seasonal lakes

▬ Rift Valley
5895 ▲ Heights in metres
375 Height of lake surface above sea level

Locator map
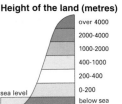

Area 580,650 km
Population 36,913,721
Capital (population) Nairobi (2,818,000)

Changes in vegetation with altitude on Mount Kenya

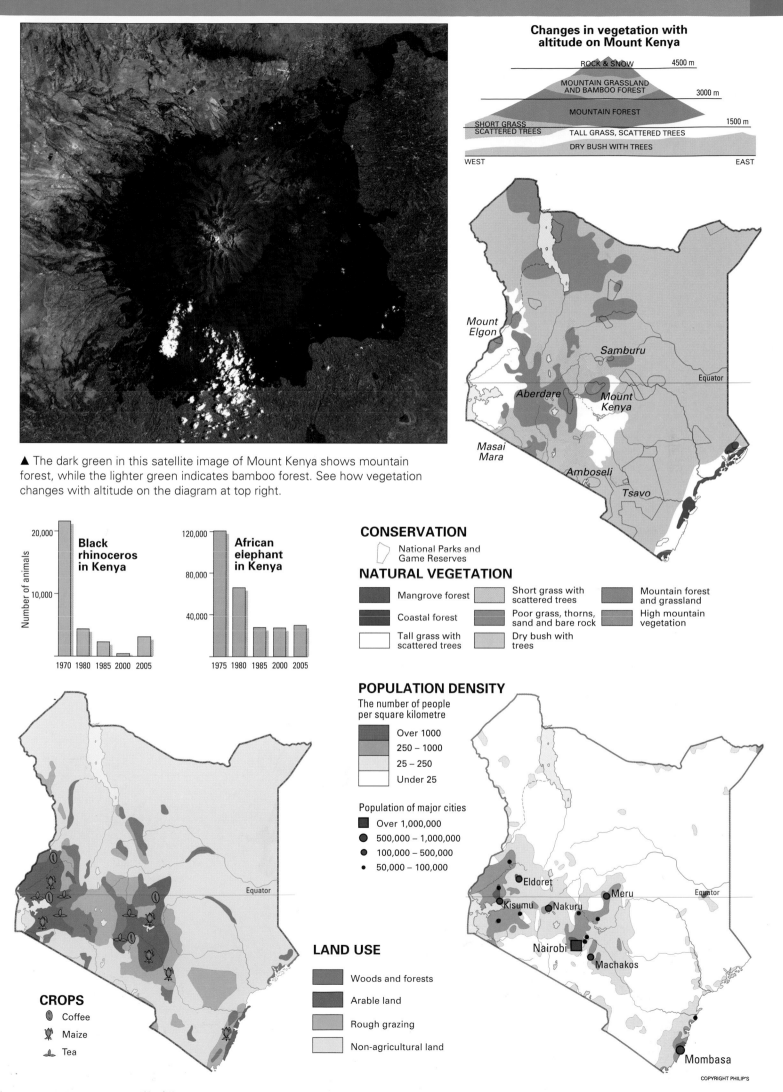

ROCK & SNOW — 4500 m

MOUNTAIN GRASSLAND AND BAMBOO FOREST — 3000 m

MOUNTAIN FOREST

SHORT GRASS SCATTERED TREES — 1500 m

TALL GRASS, SCATTERED TREES

DRY BUSH WITH TREES

WEST   EAST

Mount Elgon
Samburu
Equator
Aberdare
Mount Kenya
Masai Mara
Amboseli
Tsavo

▲ The dark green in this satellite image of Mount Kenya shows mountain forest, while the lighter green indicates bamboo forest. See how vegetation changes with altitude on the diagram at top right.

Black rhinoceros in Kenya

Number of animals

20,000

10,000

1970 1980 1985 2000 2005

African elephant in Kenya

120,000

80,000

40,000

1975 1980 1985 2000 2005

CONSERVATION

National Parks and Game Reserves

NATURAL VEGETATION

- Mangrove forest
- Coastal forest
- Tall grass with scattered trees
- Short grass with scattered trees
- Poor grass, thorns, sand and bare rock
- Dry bush with trees
- Mountain forest and grassland
- High mountain vegetation

POPULATION DENSITY

The number of people per square kilometre

- Over 1000
- 250 – 1000
- 25 – 250
- Under 25

Population of major cities

- Over 1,000,000
- 500,000 – 1,000,000
- 100,000 – 500,000
- 50,000 – 100,000

Eldoret
Meru
Equator
Kisumu
Nakuru
Nairobi
Machakos
Mombasa

LAND USE

- Woods and forests
- Arable land
- Rough grazing
- Non-agricultural land

CROPS

- Coffee
- Maize
- Tea

Equator

COPYRIGHT PHILIP'S

Cross-section along longitude 147°E   AUSTRALIA

Great Barrier Reef | Great Divide | Darling | Mount Kosciuszko 2228 | Murray | Snowy Mountains | Bass Strait | Tasmania

147°E   147°E

East from Greenwich

Height of the land (metres)

over 4000
2000-4000
1000-2000
400-1000
200-400
0-200
below sea level
sea level

Key to map symbols

■ Over 5,000,000 inhabitants

● 1,000,000 - 5,000,000 inhabitants

• Under 1,000,000 inhabitants

Canberra Capital cities underlined

— Country boundaries

— State boundaries

Seasonal lake

Seasonal rivers

Locator map

Asia — Pacific Ocean
Indian Ocean
Antarctica — Southern Ocean

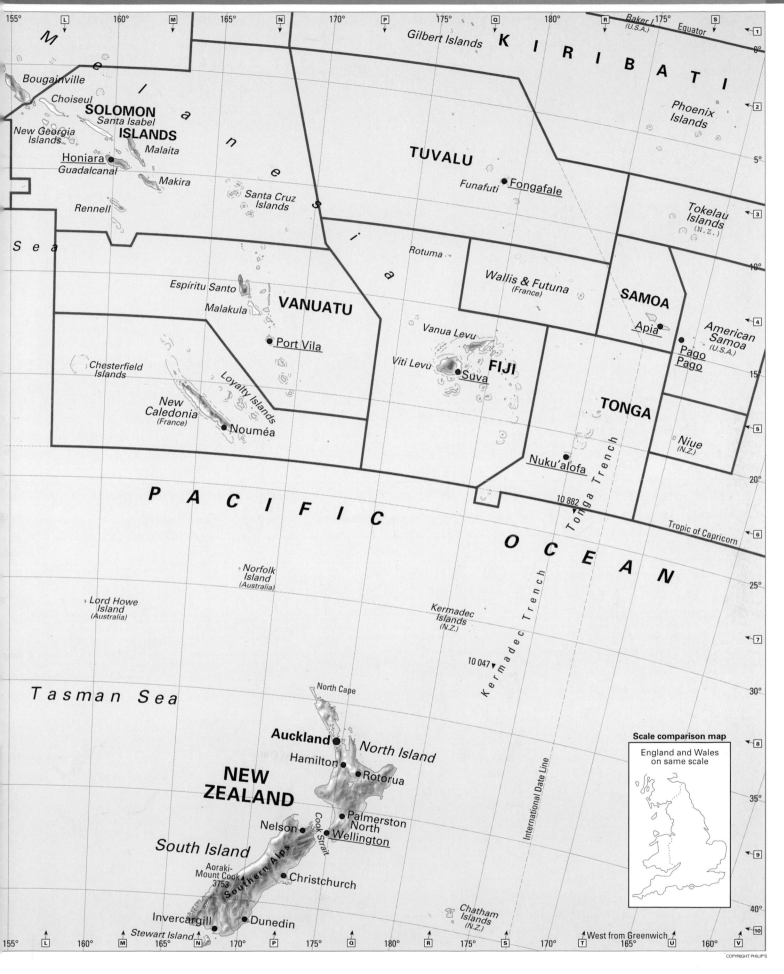

Bougainville
Choiseul
New Georgia Islands
SOLOMON ISLANDS
Santa Isabel
Malaita
Honiara
Guadalcanal
Makira
Rennell
Sea

Melanesia

KIRIBATI
Gilbert Islands
Baker I. (U.S.A.)
Equator
Phoenix Islands

TUVALU
Funafuti Fongafale
Rotuma

Tokelau Islands (N.Z.)

Espíritu Santo
Malakula
VANUATU
Port Vila

Wallis & Futuna (France)
SAMOA
Apia
American Samoa (U.S.A.)
Pago Pago

Chesterfield Islands
Loyalty Islands
New Caledonia (France)
Nouméa

Vanua Levu
Viti Levu
FIJI
Suva

TONGA

Niue (N.Z.)

Nuku'alofa
10 882

PACIFIC OCEAN

Tropic of Capricorn

Norfolk Island (Australia)

Lord Howe Island (Australia)

Kermadec Islands (N.Z.)

Tonga Trench
Kermadec Trench

10 047

Tasman Sea

North Cape

Auckland
Hamilton
Rotorua
North Island

NEW ZEALAND

Nelson
Cook Strait
Palmerston North
Wellington

South Island
Aoraki-Mount Cook 3753
Southern Alps
Christchurch

Invercargill
Stewart Island
Dunedin

International Date Line

Chatham Islands (N.Z.)

West from Greenwich

COPYRIGHT PHILIP'S

Scale comparison map

England and Wales on same scale

Scale 1:20 000 000   1 cm on the map = 200 km on the ground

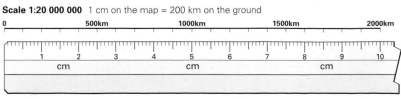

0   500km   1000km   1500km   2000km

cm   cm   cm

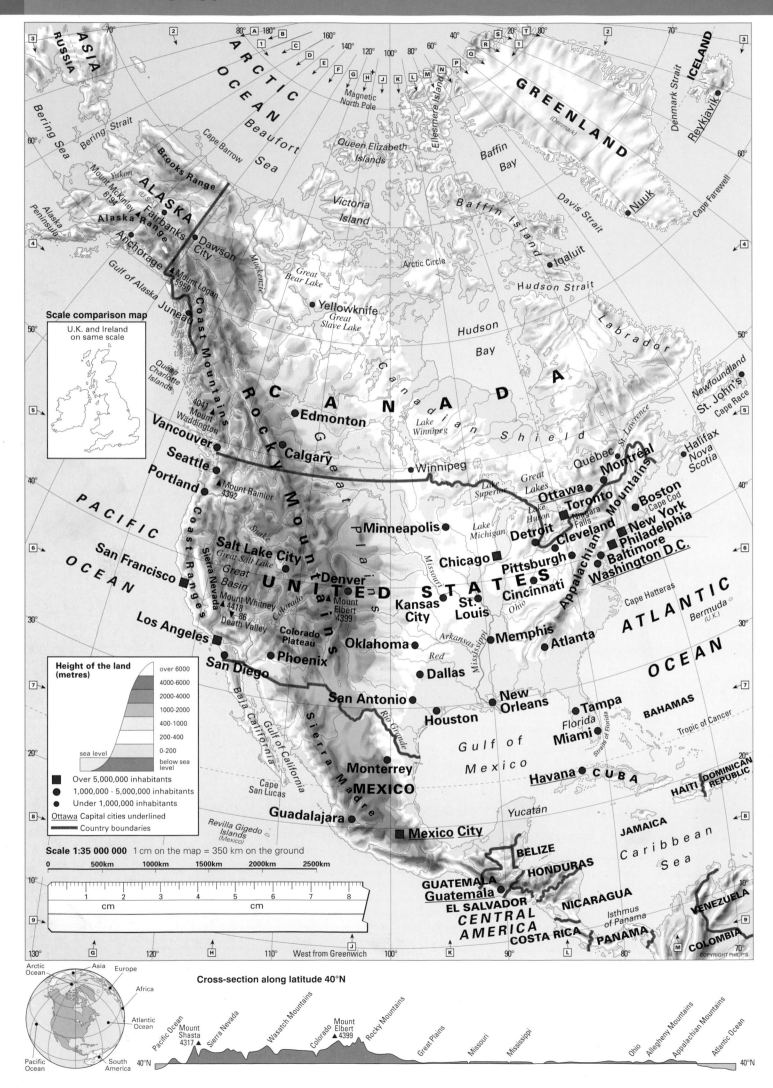

ASIA
RUSSIA

ARCTIC OCEAN

ICELAND

Bering Sea
Bering Strait
Cape Barrow
Beaufort Sea
Queen Elizabeth Islands
Ellesmere Island
GREENLAND (Denmark)

Reykjavik

Alaska Peninsula
Yukon
Mount McKinley 6194
ALASKA (U.S.A.)
Fairbanks
Brooks Range
Anchorage
Alaska Range
Dawson City
Mackenzie
Magnetic North Pole
Victoria Island
Baffin Bay
Denmark Strait
Cape Farewell

Gulf of Alaska
Mount Logan 5959
Juneau
Coast Mountains
Great Bear Lake
Yellowknife
Great Slave Lake
Hudson Bay
Arctic Circle
Baffin Island
Hudson Strait
Iqaluit
Davis Strait
Nuuk

Scale comparison map
U.K. and Ireland on same scale

Queen Charlotte Islands
Vancouver
Mount Waddington 4041
ROCKY MOUNTAINS
CANADA
Canadian Shield
Labrador
Newfoundland
St. John's
Cape Race

Seattle
Portland
Calgary
Edmonton
Lake Winnipeg
Winnipeg
Great Lakes
Lake Superior
Québec
Montréal
Halifax
Nova Scotia

PACIFIC OCEAN
Mount Rainier 4392
Snake
Minneapolis
Lake Huron
Ottawa
Toronto
Niagara Falls
Appalachian Mountains
Boston
Cape Cod

San Francisco
Salt Lake City
Great Salt Lake
Great Basin
Sierra Nevada
UNITED STATES
Chicago
Lake Michigan
Detroit
Cleveland
Pittsburgh
New York
Philadelphia
Baltimore
Washington D.C.

Coast Ranges
Mount Whitney 4418
Death Valley -86
Denver
Mount Elbert 4399
Colorado
Great Plains
Missouri
Kansas City
St. Louis
Cincinnati
Ohio
ATLANTIC OCEAN
Cape Hatteras
Bermuda (U.K.)

Los Angeles
Colorado Plateau
Oklahoma
Arkansas
Red
Mississippi
Memphis
Atlanta

San Diego
Phoenix
Dallas
Height of the land (metres)
over 6000
4000-6000
2000-4000
1000-2000
400-1000
200-400
0-200
below sea level
sea level

Baja California
Gulf of California
San Antonio
Houston
New Orleans
Gulf of Mexico
Tampa
Miami
Florida
BAHAMAS
Tropic of Cancer

Over 5,000,000 inhabitants
1,000,000 - 5,000,000 inhabitants
Under 1,000,000 inhabitants
Ottawa Capital cities underlined
Country boundaries

Cape San Lucas
Sierra Madre
Monterrey
MEXICO
Rio Grande
Havana
CUBA
HAITI
DOMINICAN REPUBLIC

Scale 1:35 000 000 1 cm on the map = 350 km on the ground
0 500km 1000km 1500km 2000km 2500km

Revilla Gigedo Islands (Mexico)
Guadalajara
Yucatán
JAMAICA
Caribbean Sea

cm cm

Mexico City
BELIZE
HONDURAS
GUATEMALA
Guatemala
EL SALVADOR
CENTRAL AMERICA
NICARAGUA
Isthmus of Panama
COSTA RICA
PANAMA
VENEZUELA
COLOMBIA

COPYRIGHT PHILIP'S

130° G 120° H 110° West from Greenwich J 100° K 90° L 80° M 70°

Arctic Ocean
Asia
Europe
Africa
Atlantic Ocean
Pacific Ocean
South America

Cross-section along latitude 40°N

40°N
Pacific Ocean
Mount Shasta 4317
Sierra Nevada
Wasatch Mountains
Colorado
Mount Elbert 4399
Rocky Mountains
Great Plains
Missouri
Mississippi
Ohio
Allegheny Mountains
Appalachian Mountains
Atlantic Ocean
40°N

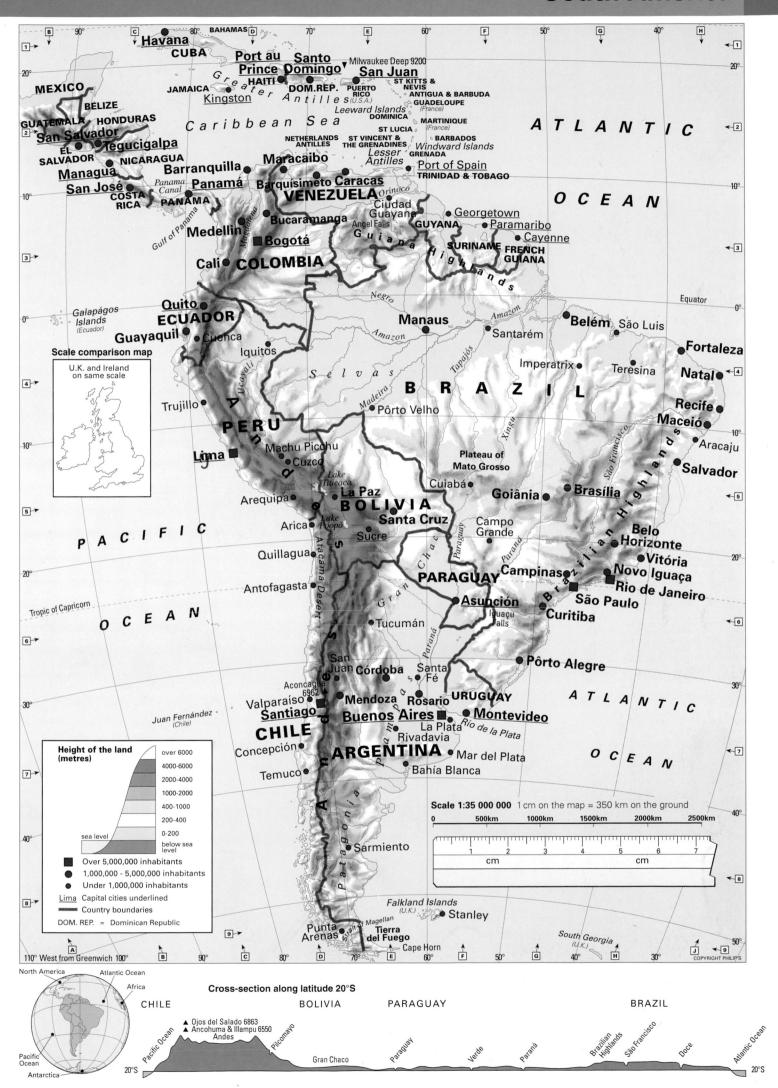

Scale comparison map
U.K. and Ireland on same scale

Height of the land (metres)

	over 6000
	4000-6000
	2000-4000
	1000-2000
	400-1000
	200-400
	0-200
	sea level
	below sea level

■ Over 5,000,000 inhabitants
● 1,000,000 - 5,000,000 inhabitants
• Under 1,000,000 inhabitants
Lima Capital cities underlined
━━ Country boundaries
DOM. REP. = Dominican Republic

Scale 1:35 000 000   1 cm on the map = 350 km on the ground

0   500km   1000km   1500km   2000km   2500km

1   2   3   4   5   6   7
cm   cm

MEXICO
BELIZE
GUATEMALA   HONDURAS
San Salvador
EL SALVADOR
Tegucigalpa
NICARAGUA
Managua
San José
COSTA RICA
PANAMA
Panamá
Panama Canal
Gulf of Panama

Havana
CUBA
BAHAMAS
Port au Prince
HAITI
JAMAICA
Kingston
Santo Domingo
DOM. REP.
San Juan
PUERTO RICO (U.S.A.)
ST KITTS & NEVIS
ANTIGUA & BARBUDA
GUADELOUPE (France)
DOMINICA
MARTINIQUE (France)
ST LUCIA
BARBADOS
ST VINCENT & THE GRENADINES
GRENADA
Windward Islands
Leeward Islands
Lesser Antilles
NETHERLANDS ANTILLES
Greater Antilles
Caribbean Sea

Milwaukee Deep 9200

ATLANTIC OCEAN

Barranquilla
Maracaibo
Barquisimeto   Caracas
VENEZUELA
Port of Spain
TRINIDAD & TOBAGO
Bucaramanga
Medellín
Bogotá
COLOMBIA
Cali
Magdalena
Ciudad Guayana
Angel Falls
Orinoco
Guiana Highlands
GUYANA
Georgetown
Paramaribo
SURINAME
Cayenne
FRENCH GUIANA

Galápagos Islands (Ecuador)

Quito
ECUADOR
Guayaquil
Cuenca
Iquitos
Trujillo
PERU
Lima
Machu Picchu
Cuzco
Arequipa
Ucayali
Negro
Amazon
Manaus
Santarém
Amazon
Selvas
Tapajós
Madeira
Pôrto Velho
BRAZIL
Belém
São Luis
Equator
Fortaleza
Natal
Recife
Maceió
Aracaju
Salvador
Imperatriz
Teresina
São Francisco
Xingu
Brazilian Highlands

Lake Titicaca
La Paz
BOLIVIA
Santa Cruz
Sucre
Arica
Lake Poopó
Quillagua
Antofagasta
Atacama Desert
PACIFIC OCEAN
Tropic of Capricorn

Cuiabá
Plateau of Mato Grosso
Goiânia
Brasília
Campo Grande
Paraguay
Paraná
PARAGUAY
Asunción
Gran Chaco
Iguaçu Falls
Campinas
São Paulo
Belo Horizonte
Vitória
Novo Iguaça
Rio de Janeiro
Curitiba
Pôrto Alegre

Juan Fernández (Chile)
Aconcagua 6962
Valparaíso
Santiago
CHILE
Concepción
Temuco
San Juan
Mendoza
Córdoba
Tucumán
Paraná
ARGENTINA
Rosario
Santa Fé
Buenos Aires
La Plata
Rivadavia
Río de la Plata
Montevideo
URUGUAY
Mar del Plata
Bahía Blanca
Pampas
Andes
Patagonia
ATLANTIC OCEAN

Sarmiento
Punta Arenas
Strait of Magellan
Tierra del Fuego
Cape Horn
Falkland Islands (U.K.)
Stanley
South Georgia (U.K.)

110° West from Greenwich 100°
COPYRIGHT PHILIP'S

North America
Atlantic Ocean
Africa
Pacific Ocean
Antarctica

Cross-section along latitude 20°S
CHILE   BOLIVIA   PARAGUAY   BRAZIL
20°S
Pacific Ocean
▲ Ojos del Salado 6863
▲ Ancohuma & Illampu 6550
Andes
Pilcomayo
Gran Chaco
Paraguay
Verde
Paraná
Brazilian Highlands
São Francisco
Doce
Atlantic Ocean
20°S

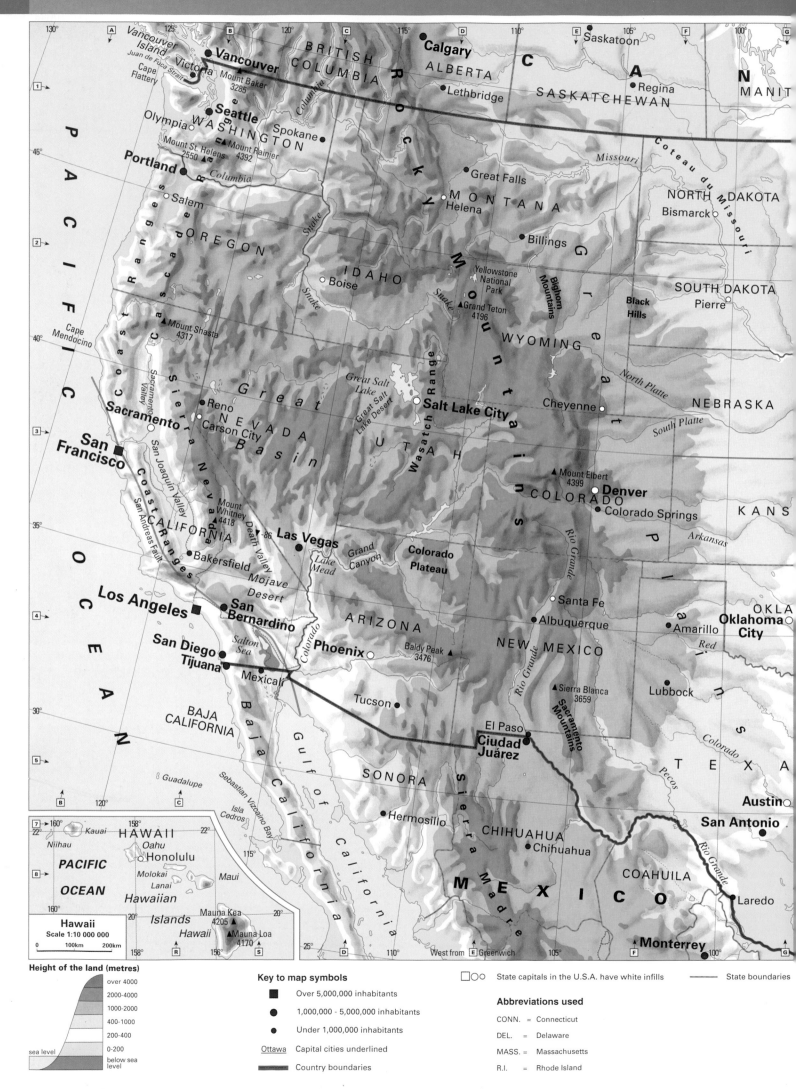

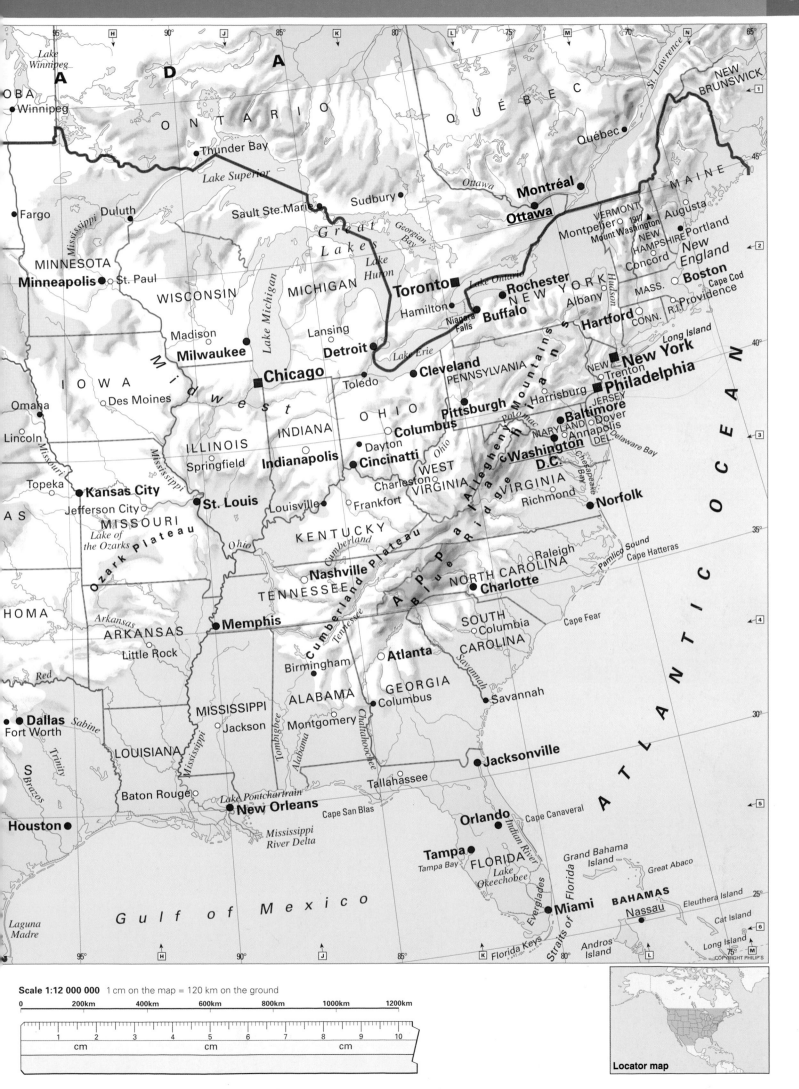

Scale 1:12 000 000   1 cm on the map = 120 km on the ground

0	200km	400km	600km	800km	1000km	1200km

Locator map

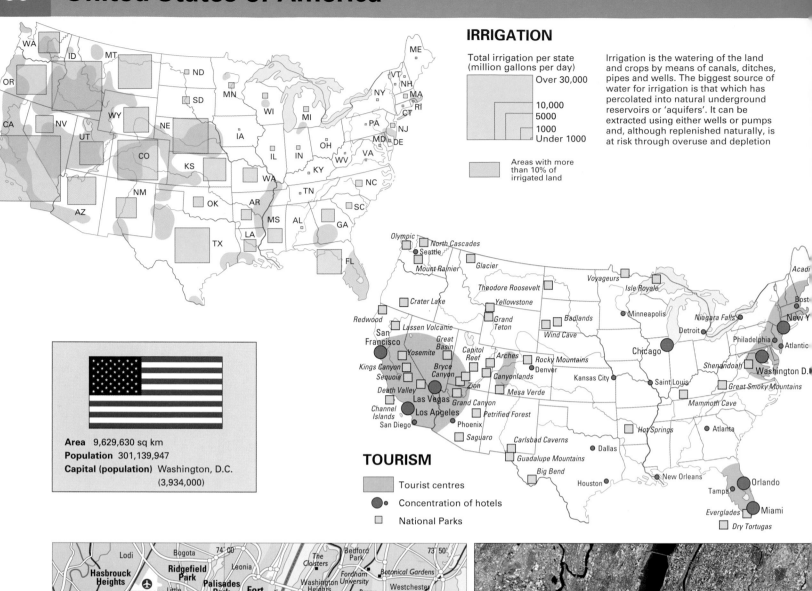

IRRIGATION

Total irrigation per state
(million gallons per day)

Over 30,000

10,000

5000

1000

Under 1000

Irrigation is the watering of the land and crops by means of canals, ditches, pipes and wells. The biggest source of water for irrigation is that which has percolated into natural underground reservoirs or 'aquifers'. It can be extracted using either wells or pumps and, although replenished naturally, is at risk through overuse and depletion

Areas with more than 10% of irrigated land

Area 9,629,630 sq km
Population 301,139,947
Capital (population) Washington, D.C.
(3,934,000)

TOURISM

Tourist centres

Concentration of hotels

National Parks

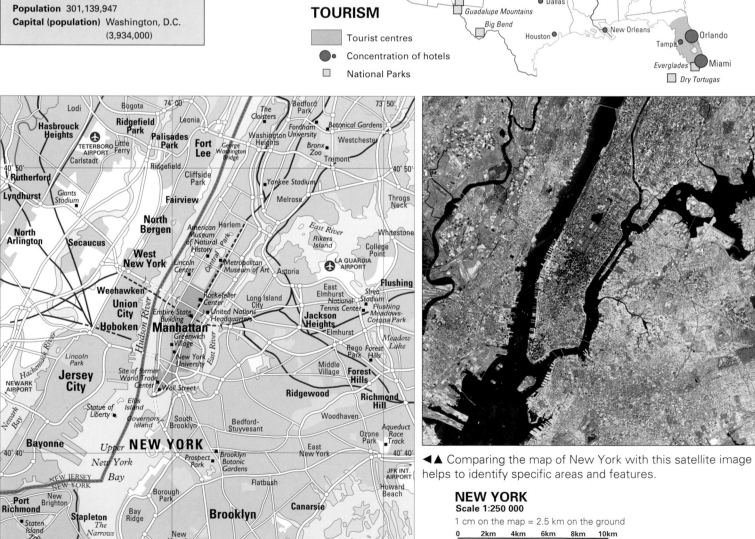

◄▲ Comparing the map of New York with this satellite image helps to identify specific areas and features.

NEW YORK
Scale 1:250 000

1 cm on the map = 2.5 km on the ground

0 2km 4km 6km 8km 10km

Central business district

Urban area

Park and open space

State boundary

Motorway

Other road

Railway

Airport

Place of interest

COPYRIGHT PHILIP'S

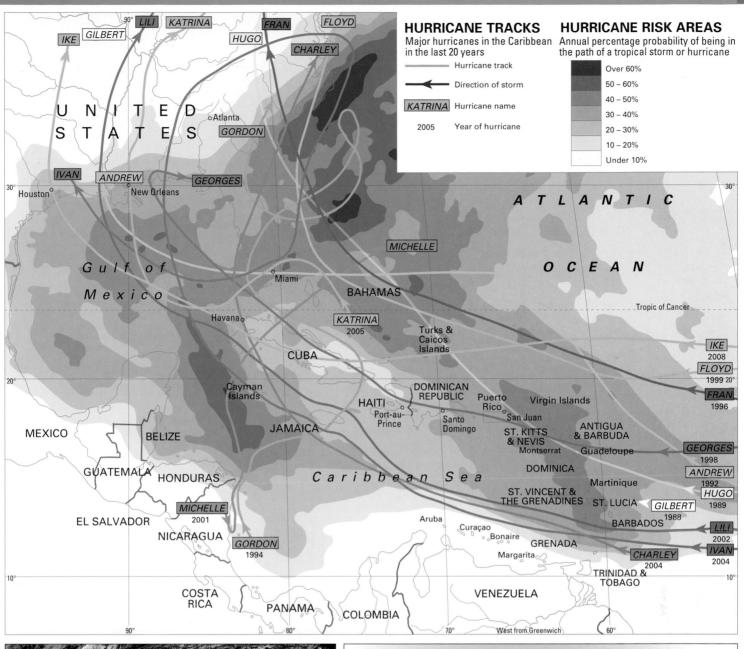

HURRICANE TRACKS
Major hurricanes in the Caribbean in the last 20 years

—— Hurricane track

⬅ Direction of storm

KATRINA Hurricane name

2005 Year of hurricane

HURRICANE RISK AREAS
Annual percentage probability of being in the path of a tropical storm or hurricane

- Over 60%
- 50 – 60%
- 40 – 50%
- 30 – 40%
- 20 – 30%
- 10 – 20%
- Under 10%

UNITED STATES

ATLANTIC OCEAN

Gulf of Mexico

Caribbean Sea

▲ Hurricane Katrina hit the USA's Gulf Coast on 29 August 2005. It was the costliest and one of the five deadliest hurricanes ever to strike the United States. This satellite image shows the storm approaching the US coastline.

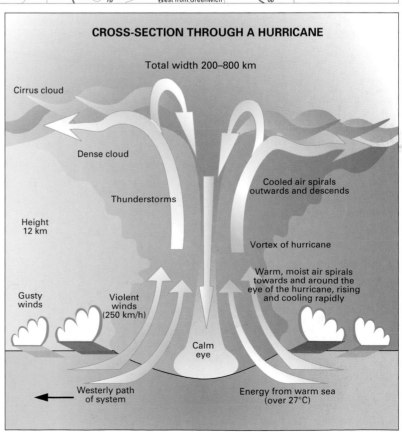

CROSS-SECTION THROUGH A HURRICANE

Total width 200–800 km

Cirrus cloud

Dense cloud

Thunderstorms

Cooled air spirals outwards and descends

Vortex of hurricane

Height 12 km

Warm, moist air spirals towards and around the eye of the hurricane, rising and cooling rapidly

Gusty winds

Violent winds (250 km/h)

Calm eye

Westerly path of system

Energy from warm sea (over 27°C)

Scale comparison map

England and Wales
on same scale

Height of the land (metres)

| over 4000 |
| 2000-4000 |
| 1000-2000 |
| 400-1000 |
| 200-400 |
| 0-200 |
| below sea level |

sea level

Key to map symbols

■ Over 5,000,000 inhabitants

● 1,000,000 - 5,000,000 inhabitants

• Under 1,000,000 inhabitants

Mexico   Capital cities underlined

──── Country boundaries

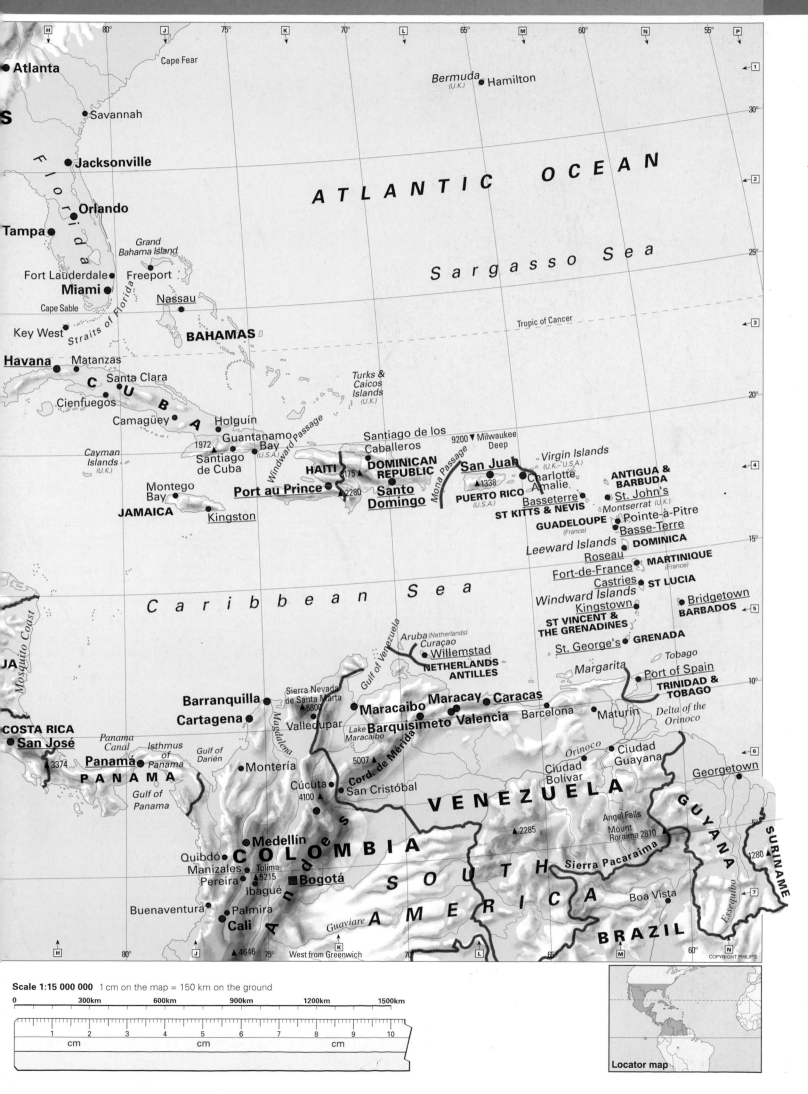

Scale 1:15 000 000   1 cm on the map = 150 km on the ground

| 0 | 300km | 600km | 900km | 1200km | 1500km |

Locator map

Scale 1:21 000 000   1 cm on the map = 210 km on the ground

0   210km   420km   630km   840km   1050km   1260km

cm

Height of the land (metres)

over 4000
2000 – 4000
1000 – 2000
400 – 1000
200 – 400
0 – 200
below sea level

sea level

Key to map symbols

■ Over 5,000,000 inhabitants
● 1,000,000 – 5,000,000 inhabitants
• Under 1,000,000 inhabitants

Brasília Capital cities underlined
—— Country boundaries
——— State boundaries

Area 8,514,215 sq km
Population 190,011,000
Capital (population) Brasília (3,341,000)

COPYRIGHT PHILIP'S

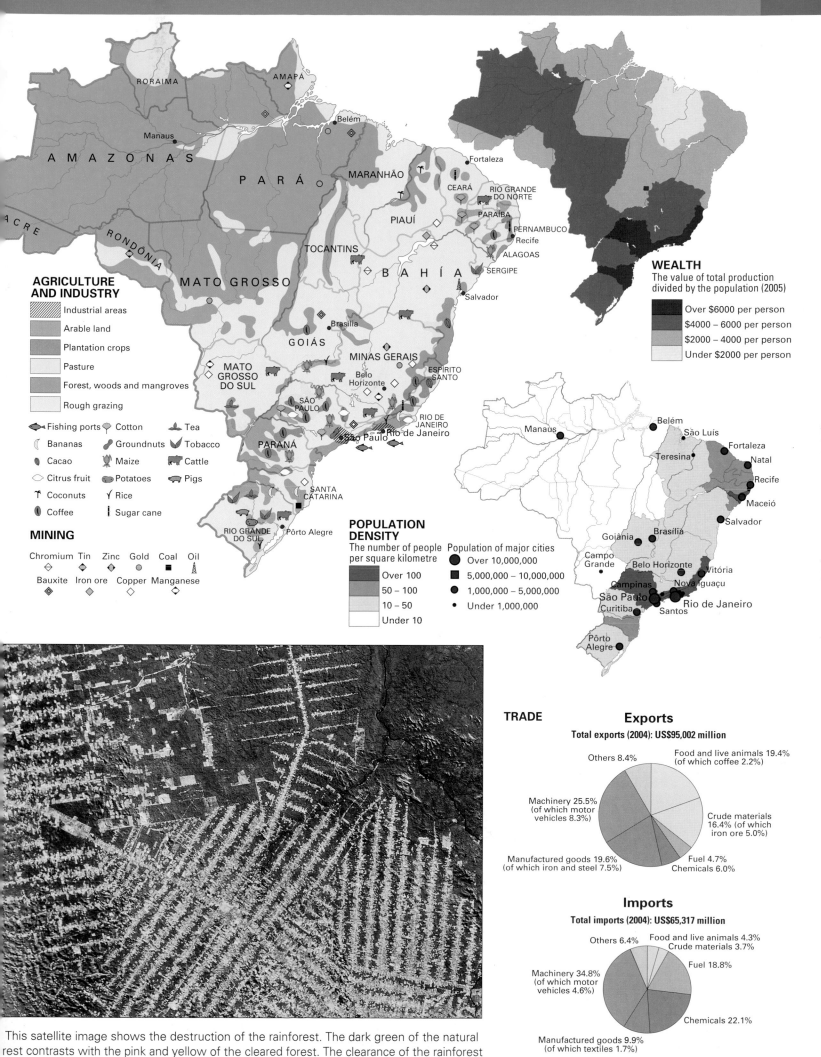

AGRICULTURE AND INDUSTRY

- Industrial areas
- Arable land
- Plantation crops
- Pasture
- Forest, woods and mangroves
- Rough grazing

- Fishing ports
- Bananas
- Cacao
- Citrus fruit
- Coconuts
- Coffee
- Cotton
- Groundnuts
- Maize
- Potatoes
- Rice
- Sugar cane
- Tea
- Tobacco
- Cattle
- Pigs

MINING

Chromium Tin Zinc Gold Coal Oil
Bauxite Iron ore Copper Manganese

POPULATION DENSITY

The number of people per square kilometre

- Over 100
- 50 – 100
- 10 – 50
- Under 10

Population of major cities
- Over 10,000,000
- 5,000,000 – 10,000,000
- 1,000,000 – 5,000,000
- Under 1,000,000

WEALTH

The value of total production divided by the population (2005)

- Over $6000 per person
- $4000 – 6000 per person
- $2000 – 4000 per person
- Under $2000 per person

TRADE

Exports

Total exports (2004): US$95,002 million

- Others 8.4%
- Food and live animals 19.4% (of which coffee 2.2%)
- Crude materials 16.4% (of which iron ore 5.0%)
- Fuel 4.7%
- Chemicals 6.0%
- Manufactured goods 19.6% (of which iron and steel 7.5%)
- Machinery 25.5% (of which motor vehicles 8.3%)

Imports

Total imports (2004): US$65,317 million

- Others 6.4%
- Food and live animals 4.3%
- Crude materials 3.7%
- Fuel 18.8%
- Chemicals 22.1%
- Manufactured goods 9.9% (of which textiles 1.7%)
- Machinery 34.8% (of which motor vehicles 4.6%)

This satellite image shows the destruction of the rainforest. The dark green of the natural rest contrasts with the pink and yellow of the cleared forest. The clearance of the rainforest not only for timber, but also to grow soya, palm oil and other crops, and to raise cattle.

North
Magnetic Pole
+ 2007

North
Pole

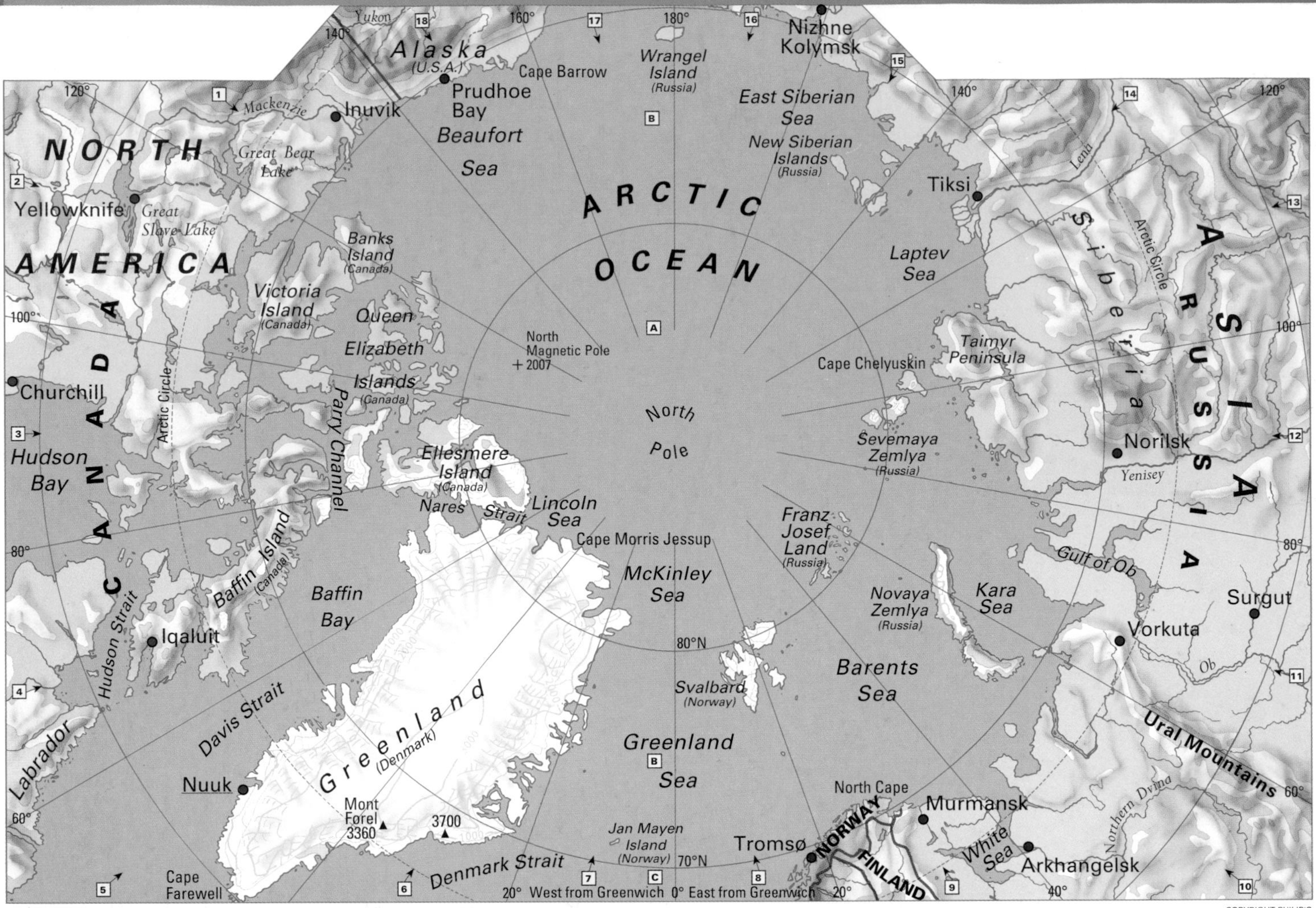

Height of the land (metres)

over 4000	
2000-4000	
1000-2000	
400-1000	
200-400	
0-200	
sea level	
below sea level	

Key to map symbols

Height of ice (in metres)

Land permanently covered with ice

● Under 1,000,000 inhabitants

Nuuk Capital cities underlined

■ Davis Selected research station and
(Australia) the country which runs it

◄This image shows the
September minimum extent
of the Arctic sea ice in 2008.
The general trend over
recent years has been the
reduction of the ice area.
One by-product of this is the
opening-up of clear sea, which
would enable shipping to move
between the Atlantic and Pacific
Oceans more easily.

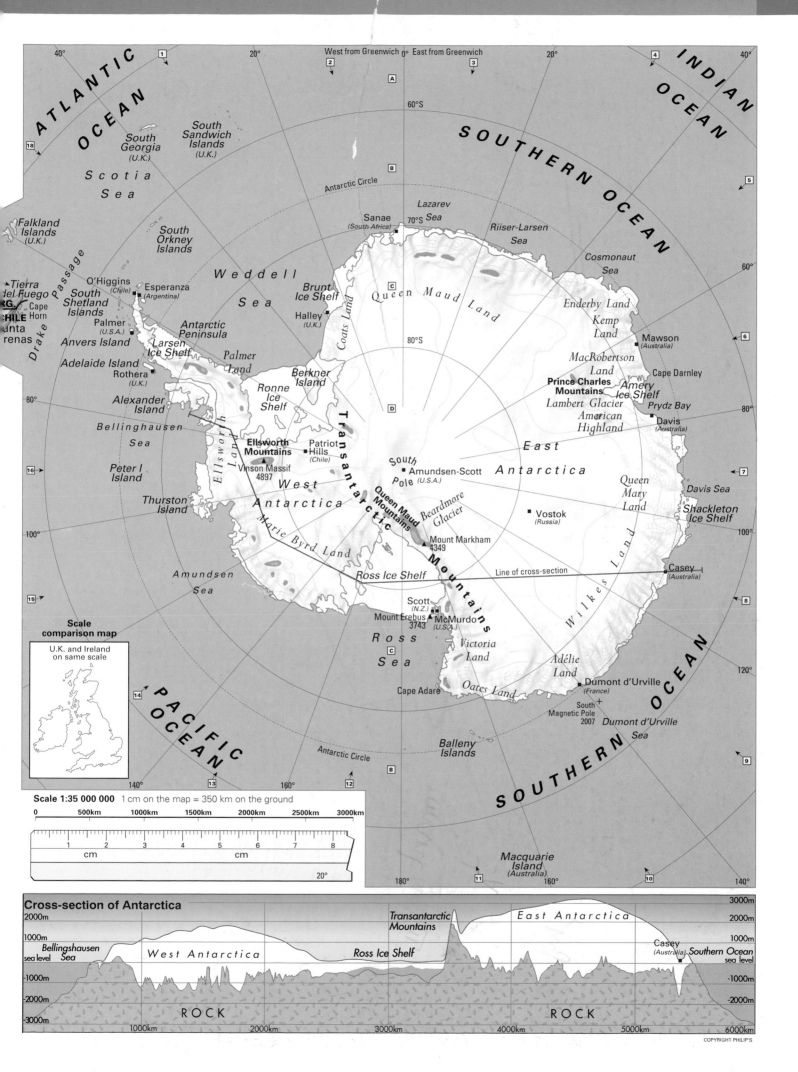

ATLANTIC OCEAN

INDIAN OCEAN

SOUTHERN OCEAN

West from Greenwich East from Greenwich

Scotia Sea

South Georgia (U.K.)

South Sandwich Islands (U.K.)

60°S

Antarctic Circle

Lazarev Sea

Sanae (South Africa)

70°S

Riiser-Larsen Sea

Cosmonaut Sea

Falkland Islands (U.K.)

South Orkney Islands

Weddell Sea

Brunt Ice Shelf

Halley (U.K.)

Queen Maud Land

Enderby Land

Kemp Land

80°S

MacRobertson Land

Mawson (Australia)

Cape Darnley

Tierra del Fuego

O'Higgins (Chile)

Esperanza (Argentina)

Coats Land

Berkner Island

Prince Charles Mountains

Amery Ice Shelf

Prydz Bay

Cape Horn

Palmer (U.S.A.)

Antarctic Peninsula

Larsen Ice Shelf

Palmer Land

Lambert Glacier

American Highland

Davis (Australia)

Punta Arenas

Anvers Island

Ronne Ice Shelf

East Antarctica

80°

Adelaide Island

Rothera (U.K.)

Alexander Island

Ellsworth Mountains

Patriot Hills (Chile)

South Pole

Amundsen-Scott (U.S.A.)

Queen Mary Land

Bellinghausen Sea

Vinson Massif 4897

West Antarctica

Queen Maud Mountains

Beardmore Glacier

Vostok (Russia)

Davis Sea

Shackleton Ice Shelf

Peter I Island

Thurston Island

Marie Byrd Land

Mount Markham 4349

Line of cross-section

Casey (Australia)

Amundsen Sea

Ross Ice Shelf

Scott (N.Z.)

McMurdo (U.S.A.)

Wilkes Land

Mount Erebus 3743

Ross Sea

Victoria Land

Adélie Land

Dumont d'Urville (France)

Cape Adare

Oates Land

South Magnetic Pole 2007

Dumont d'Urville Sea

Balleny Islands

Antarctic Circle

Macquarie Island (Australia)

Scale comparison map

U.K. and Ireland on same scale

PACIFIC OCEAN

SOUTHERN OCEAN

Scale 1:35 000 000 1 cm on the map = 350 km on the ground

| 0 | 500km | 1000km | 1500km | 2000km | 2500km | 3000km |

cm   cm

20°

Cross-section of Antarctica

3000m

Transantarctic Mountains

East Antarctica

2000m

Bellinghausen Sea

West Antarctica

Ross Ice Shelf

Casey (Australia)

Southern Ocean

sea level

1000m

-1000m

-2000m

-3000m

ROCK

ROCK

1000km   2000km   3000km   4000km   5000km   6000km

COPYRIGHT PHILIP'S

CONTINENT	AREA '000 kilometres	COLDEST PLACE degrees Celsius		HOTTEST PLACE degrees Celsius		WETTEST PLACE average annual rainfall, mm		DRIEST PLACE average annual rainfall, mm	
Asia	44,500	Oymyakon, Russia –70°C	①	Tirat Zevi, Israel 54°C	⑧	Mawsynram, India 11,870	⑮	Aden, Yemen 46	㉑
Africa	30,302	Ifrane, Morocco –24°C	②	Al Aziziyah, Libya 58°C	⑨	Debundscha, Cameroon 10, 290	⑯	Wadi Haifa, Sudan 2	㉒
North America	24,241	Snag, Yukon –63°C	③	Death Valley, California 57°C	⑩	Henderson Lake, Canada 6,500	⑰	Bataques, Mexico 30	㉓
South America	17,793	Sarmiento, Argentina –33°C	④	Rivadavia, Argentina 49°C	⑪	Quibdó, Colombia 8,990	⑱	Quillagua, Chile 0.6	㉔
Antarctica	14,000	Vostok –89°C	⑤	Vanda Station 15°C	⑫				
Europe	9,957	Ust Shchugor, Russia –55°C	⑥	Seville, Spain 50°C	⑬	Crkvice, Montenegro 4,650	⑲	Astrakhan, Russia 160	㉕
Oceania	8,557	Charlotte Pass, Australia –22°C	⑦	Oodnadatta, Australia 51°C	⑭	Tully, Australia 4,550	⑳	Mulka, Australia 100	㉖

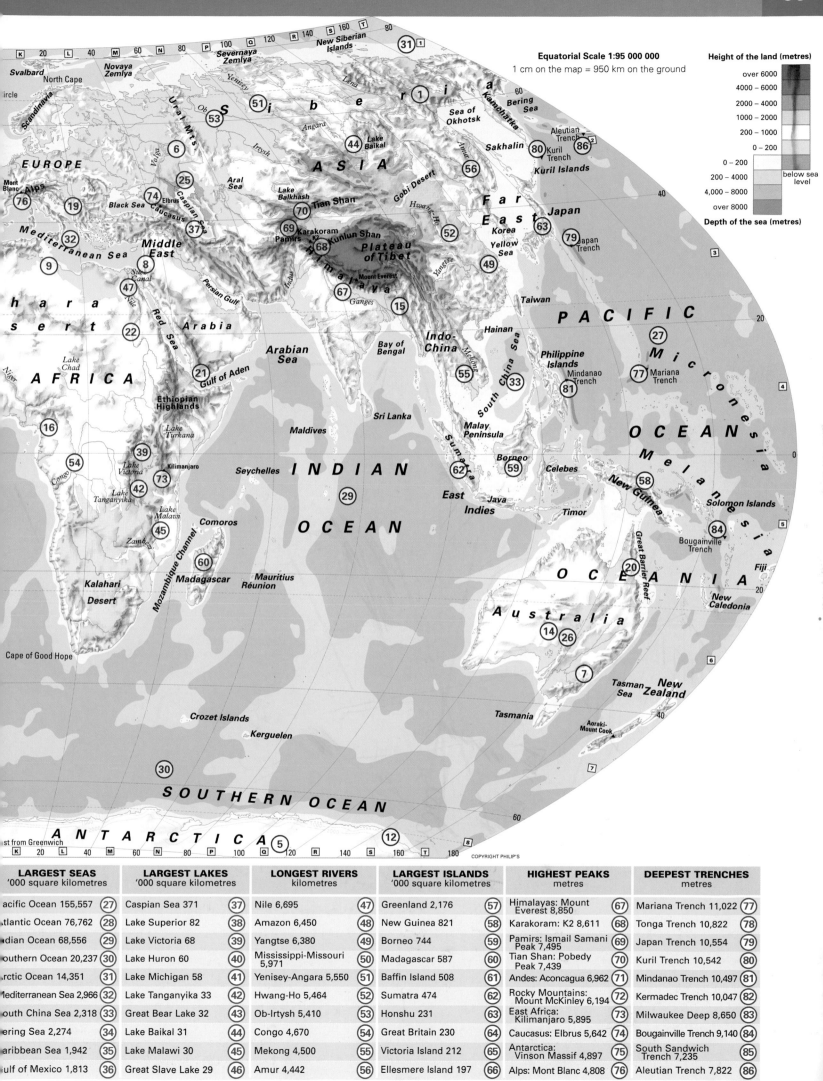

Equatorial Scale 1:95 000 000
1 cm on the map = 950 km on the ground

Height of the land (metres)
- over 6000
- 4000 – 6000
- 2000 – 4000
- 1000 – 2000
- 200 – 1000
- 0 – 200

- 0 – 200
- 200 – 4000
- 4,000 – 8,000
- over 8000

below sea level

Depth of the sea (metres)

COPYRIGHT PHILIP'S

LARGEST SEAS '000 square kilometres		LARGEST LAKES '000 square kilometres		LONGEST RIVERS kilometres		LARGEST ISLANDS '000 square kilometres		HIGHEST PEAKS metres		DEEPEST TRENCHES metres	
Pacific Ocean 155,557	(27)	Caspian Sea 371	(37)	Nile 6,695	(47)	Greenland 2,176	(57)	Himalayas: Mount Everest 8,850	(67)	Mariana Trench 11,022	(77)
Atlantic Ocean 76,762	(28)	Lake Superior 82	(38)	Amazon 6,450	(48)	New Guinea 821	(58)	Karakoram: K2 8,611	(68)	Tonga Trench 10,822	(78)
Indian Ocean 68,556	(29)	Lake Victoria 68	(39)	Yangtse 6,380	(49)	Borneo 744	(59)	Pamirs: Ismail Samani Peak 7,495	(69)	Japan Trench 10,554	(79)
Southern Ocean 20,237	(30)	Lake Huron 60	(40)	Mississippi-Missouri 5,971	(50)	Madagascar 587	(60)	Tian Shan: Pobedy Peak 7,439	(70)	Kuril Trench 10,542	(80)
Arctic Ocean 14,351	(31)	Lake Michigan 58	(41)	Yenisey-Angara 5,550	(51)	Baffin Island 508	(61)	Andes: Aconcagua 6,962	(71)	Mindanao Trench 10,497	(81)
Mediterranean Sea 2,966	(32)	Lake Tanganyika 33	(42)	Hwang-Ho 5,464	(52)	Sumatra 474	(62)	Rocky Mountains: Mount McKinley 6,194	(72)	Kermadec Trench 10,047	(82)
South China Sea 2,318	(33)	Great Bear Lake 32	(43)	Ob-Irtysh 5,410	(53)	Honshu 231	(63)	East Africa: Kilimanjaro 5,895	(73)	Milwaukee Deep 8,650	(83)
Bering Sea 2,274	(34)	Lake Baikal 31	(44)	Congo 4,670	(54)	Great Britain 230	(64)	Caucasus: Elbrus 5,642	(74)	Bougainville Trench 9,140	(84)
Caribbean Sea 1,942	(35)	Lake Malawi 30	(45)	Mekong 4,500	(55)	Victoria Island 212	(65)	Antarctica: Vinson Massif 4,897	(75)	South Sandwich Trench 7,235	(85)
Gulf of Mexico 1,813	(36)	Great Slave Lake 29	(46)	Amur 4,442	(56)	Ellesmere Island 197	(66)	Alps: Mont Blanc 4,808	(76)	Aleutian Trench 7,822	(86)

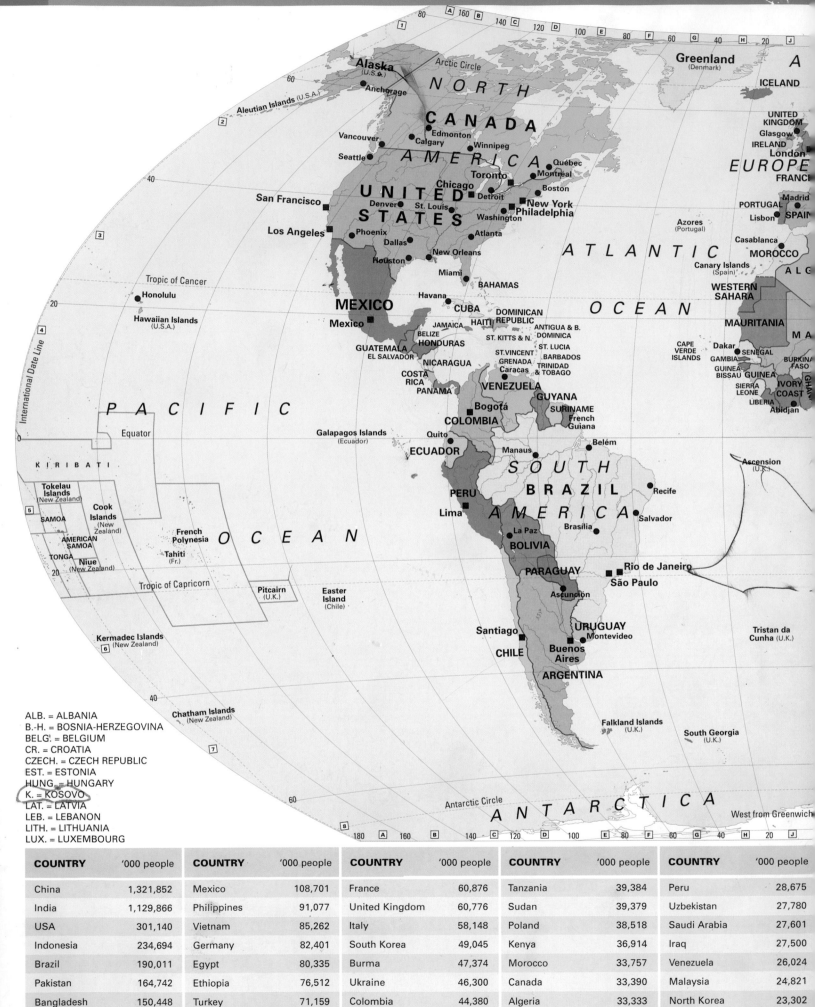

ALB. = ALBANIA
B.-H. = BOSNIA-HERZEGOVINA
BELG. = BELGIUM
CR. = CROATIA
CZECH. = CZECH REPUBLIC
EST. = ESTONIA
HUNG. = HUNGARY
K. = KOSOVO
LAT. = LATVIA
LEB. = LEBANON
LITH. = LITHUANIA
LUX. = LUXEMBOURG

COUNTRY	'000 people	COUNTRY	'000 people	COUNTRY	'000 people	COUNTRY	'000 people	COUNTRY	'000 people
China	1,321,852	Mexico	108,701	France	60,876	Tanzania	39,384	Peru	28,675
India	1,129,866	Philippines	91,077	United Kingdom	60,776	Sudan	39,379	Uzbekistan	27,780
USA	301,140	Vietnam	85,262	Italy	58,148	Poland	38,518	Saudi Arabia	27,601
Indonesia	234,694	Germany	82,401	South Korea	49,045	Kenya	36,914	Iraq	27,500
Brazil	190,011	Egypt	80,335	Burma	47,374	Morocco	33,757	Venezuela	26,024
Pakistan	164,742	Ethiopia	76,512	Ukraine	46,300	Canada	33,390	Malaysia	24,821
Bangladesh	150,448	Turkey	71,159	Colombia	44,380	Algeria	33,333	North Korea	23,302
Russia	141,378	Congo (Dem. Rep.)	65,752	South Africa	43,998	Afghanistan	31,890	Ghana	22,931
Nigeria	135,031	Iran	65,398	Spain	40,448	Uganda	30,263	Taiwan	22,859
Japan	127,434	Thailand	65,068	Argentina	40,302	Nepal	28,902	Romania	22,276

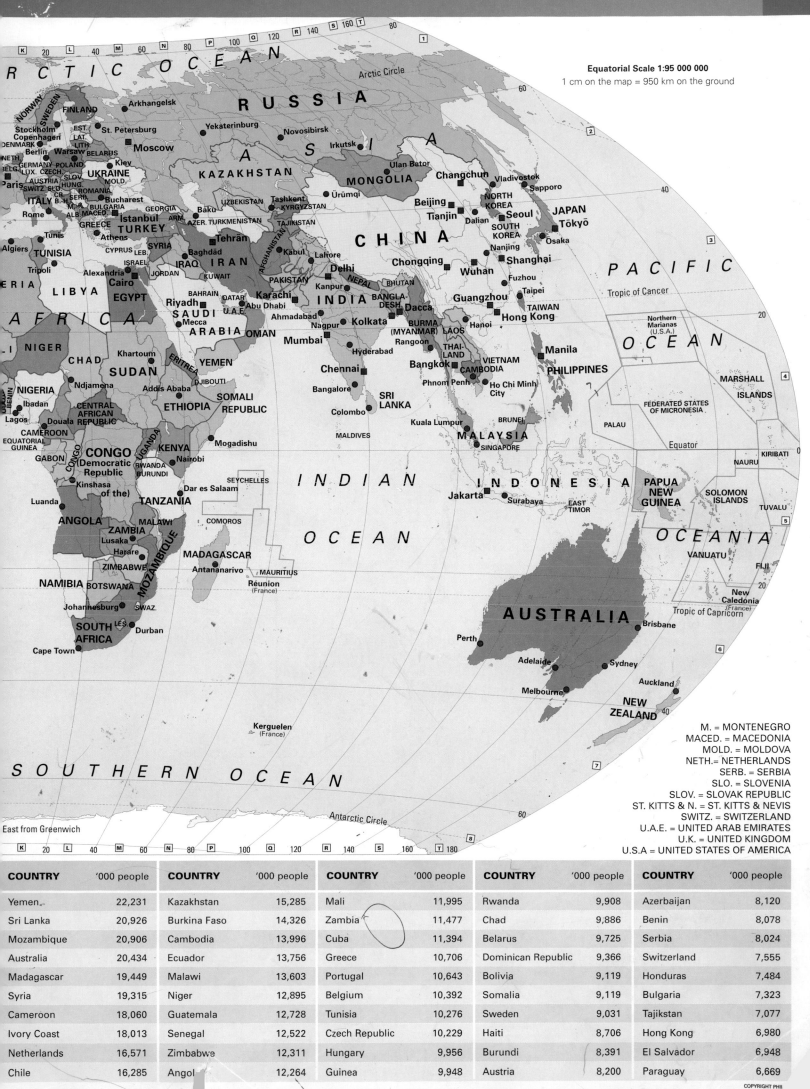

M. = MONTENEGRO
MACED. = MACEDONIA
MOLD.= MOLDOVA
NETH.= NETHERLANDS
SERB. = SERBIA
SLO. = SLOVENIA
SLOV. = SLOVAK REPUBLIC
ST. KITTS & N.= ST. KITTS & NEVIS
SWITZ. = SWITZERLAND
U.A.E. = UNITED ARAB EMIRATES
U.K. = UNITED KINGDOM
U.S.A = UNITED STATES OF AMERICA

COUNTRY	'000 people	COUNTRY	'000 people	COUNTRY	'000 people	COUNTRY	'000 people	COUNTRY	'000 people
Yemen	22,231	Kazakhstan	15,285	Mali	11,995	Rwanda	9,908	Azerbaijan	8,120
Sri Lanka	20,926	Burkina Faso	14,326	Zambia	11,477	Chad	9,886	Benin	8,078
Mozambique	20,906	Cambodia	13,996	Cuba	11,394	Belarus	9,725	Serbia	8,024
Australia	20,434	Ecuador	13,756	Greece	10,706	Dominican Republic	9,366	Switzerland	7,555
Madagascar	19,449	Malawi	13,603	Portugal	10,643	Bolivia	9,119	Honduras	7,484
Syria	19,315	Niger	12,895	Belgium	10,392	Somalia	9,119	Bulgaria	7,323
Cameroon	18,060	Guatemala	12,728	Tunisia	10,276	Sweden	9,031	Tajikstan	7,077
Ivory Coast	18,013	Senegal	12,522	Czech Republic	10,229	Haiti	8,706	Hong Kong	6,980
Netherlands	16,571	Zimbabwe	12,311	Hungary	9,956	Burundi	8,391	El Salvador	6,948
Chile	16,285	Angol	12,264	Guinea	9,948	Austria	8,200	Paraguay	6,669

CLIMATE REGIONS

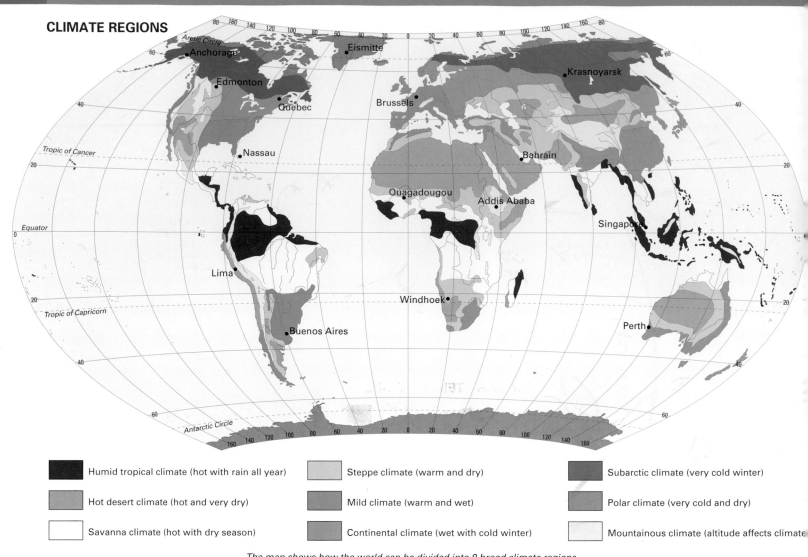

■ Humid tropical climate (hot with rain all year)	▨ Steppe climate (warm and dry)	▨ Subarctic climate (very cold winter)
▨ Hot desert climate (hot and very dry)	▨ Mild climate (warm and wet)	▨ Polar climate (very cold and dry)
□ Savanna climate (hot with dry season)	▨ Continental climate (wet with cold winter)	▨ Mountainous climate (altitude affects climate)

The map shows how the world can be divided into 9 broad climate regions.

CLIMATE GRAPHS

The graphs below give examples of places within each climate region, showing how temperature and rainfall vary from month to month.

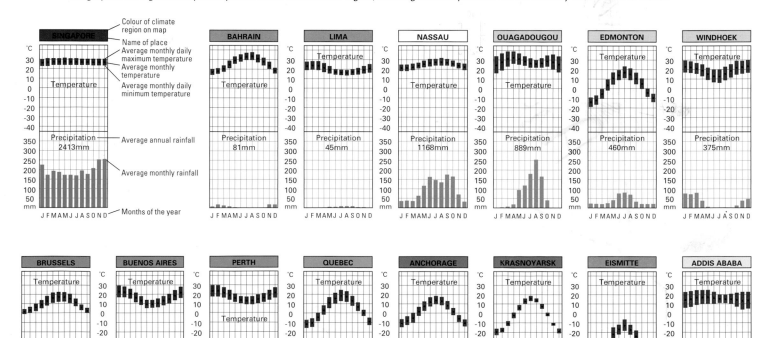

HUMID TROPICAL CLIMATE

HOT DESERT CLIMATE

SAVANNA

MILD CLIMATE

POLAR CLIMATE

MOUNTAINOUS CLIMATE

ANNUAL RAINFALL

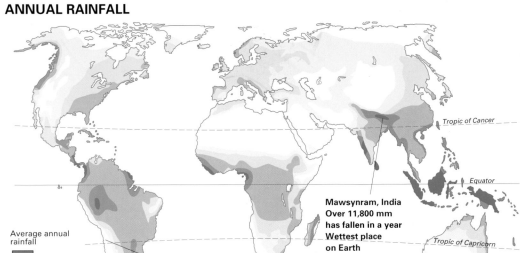

Mawsynram, India
Over 11,800 mm
has fallen in a year
Wettest place
on Earth

Atacama Desert
Driest place on Earth
No rain has ever
been recorded

Average annual rainfall

3000 mm
2000 mm
1000 mm
500 mm
250 mm

JANUARY TEMPERATURE

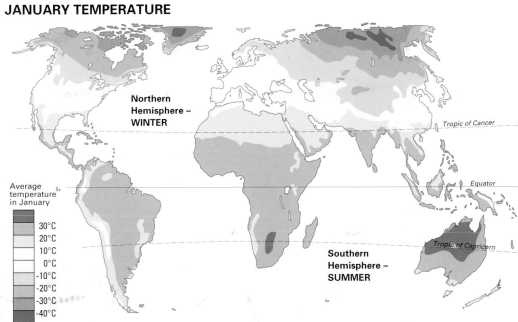

Northern Hemisphere – WINTER

Southern Hemisphere – SUMMER

Average temperature in January

30°C
20°C
10°C
0°C
-10°C
-20°C
-30°C
-40°C

JULY TEMPERATURE

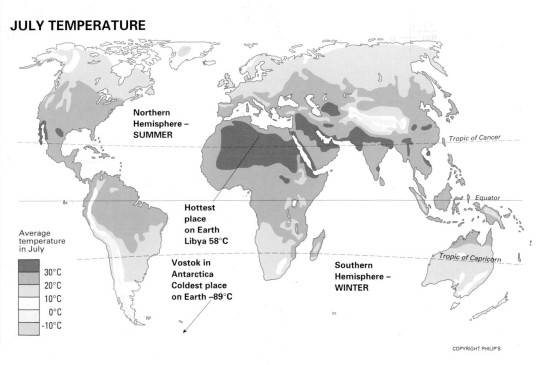

Northern Hemisphere – SUMMER

Hottest place on Earth Libya 58°C

Vostok in Antarctica Coldest place on Earth –89°C

Southern Hemisphere – WINTER

Average temperature in July

30°C
20°C
10°C
0°C
-10°C

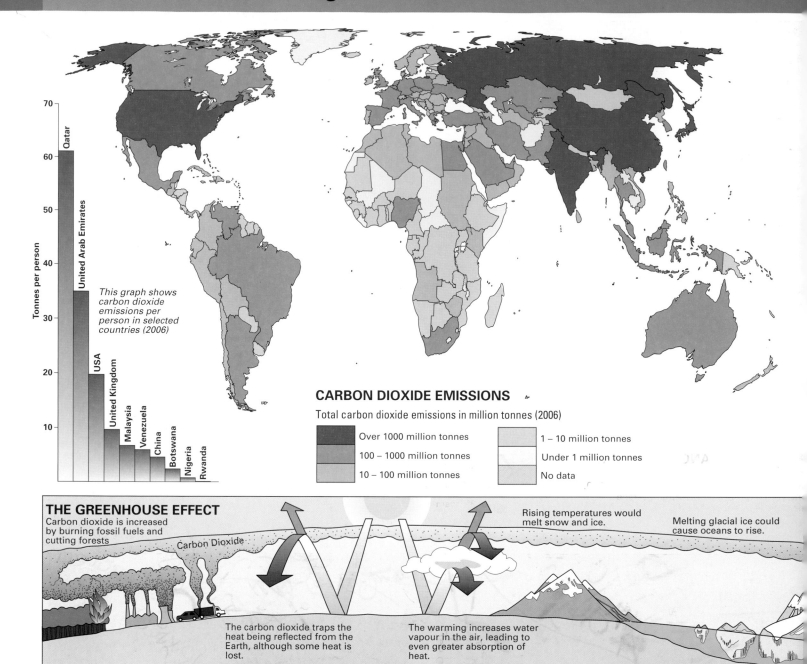

This graph shows carbon dioxide emissions per person in selected countries (2006)

Tonnes per person

Qatar
United Arab Emirates
USA
United Kingdom
Malaysia
Venezuela
China
Botswana
Nigeria
Rwanda

CARBON DIOXIDE EMISSIONS

Total carbon dioxide emissions in million tonnes (2006)

Over 1000 million tonnes	1 – 10 million tonnes
100 – 1000 million tonnes	Under 1 million tonnes
10 – 100 million tonnes	No data

THE GREENHOUSE EFFECT

Carbon dioxide is increased by burning fossil fuels and cutting forests

Carbon Dioxide

Rising temperatures would melt snow and ice.

Melting glacial ice could cause oceans to rise.

The carbon dioxide traps the heat being reflected from the Earth, although some heat is lost.

The warming increases water vapour in the air, leading to even greater absorption of heat.

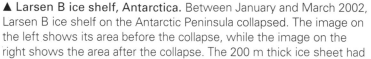

▲ **Larsen B ice shelf, Antarctica.** Between January and March 2002, Larsen B ice shelf on the Antarctic Peninsula collapsed. The image on the left shows its area before the collapse, while the image on the right shows the area after the collapse. The 200 m thick ice sheet had been retreating before this date, but over 500 billion tonnes of ice collapsed in under a month. This was due to rising temperatures of 0.5°C per year in this part of Antarctica. Satellite images like these are the only way for scientists to monitor inaccessible areas of the world.

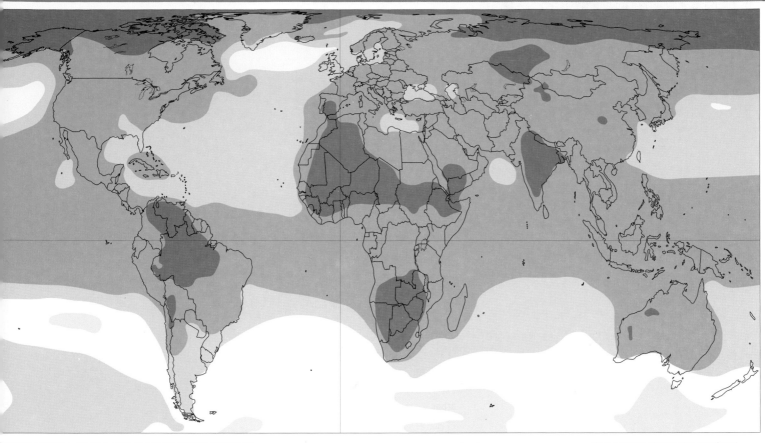

PREDICTED CHANGE IN TEMPERATURE

The difference between actual annual
average surface air temperature, 1969–1990,
and predicted annual average surface
air temperature, 2070–2100

■ 5 – 10°C warmer	□ 1 – 2°C warmer
■ 3 – 5°C warmer	□ 0 – 1°C warmer
□ 2 – 3°C warmer	

*These maps shows the predicted
increase assuming a 'medium growth'
of the global economy and assuming
that no measures to combat the
emission of greenhouse gases
are taken.*

*It should be noted that these predicted
annual average changes mask quite
significant seasonal detail.*

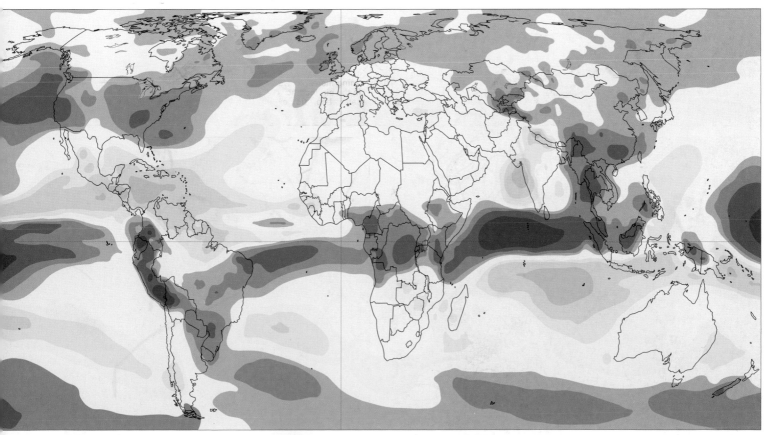

PREDICTED CHANGE IN RAINFALL

The difference between actual annual average
rainfall, 1969–1990, and predicted annual
average rainfall, 2070–2100

■ Over 2 mm more rain per day	□ 0.2 – 0.5 mm more rain per day	□ 0.5 – 1 mm less rain per day
■ 1 – 2 mm more rain per day	□ No change	□ 1 – 2 mm less rain per day
■ Over 2 mm more rain per day	□ 0.2 – 0.5 mm less rain per day	□ Over 2 mm less rain per day

Source: The Hadley Centre of Climate Prediction
and Research, Met Office

COPYRIGHT PHILIP'S

TUNDRA AND MOUNTAIN VEGETATION

NEEDLELEAF EVERGREEN FOREST

MID-LATITUDE GRASSLAND

TROPICAL BROADLEAF RAINFOREST

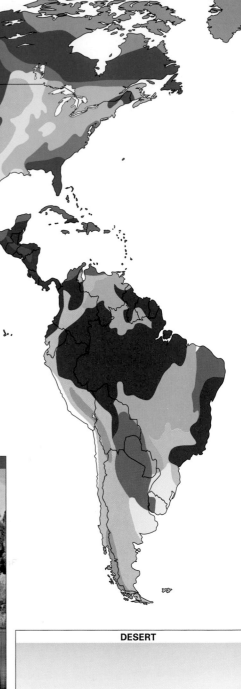

DESERT

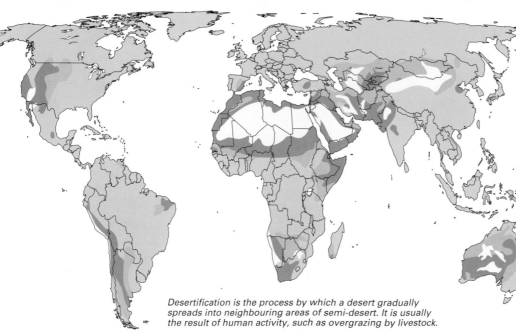

Desertification is the process by which a desert gradually spreads into neighbouring areas of semi-desert. It is usually the result of human activity, such as overgrazing by livestock.

DESERTIFICATION

☐ Existing desert

▨ Areas with a high risk of desertification

▨ Areas with a moderate risk of desertification

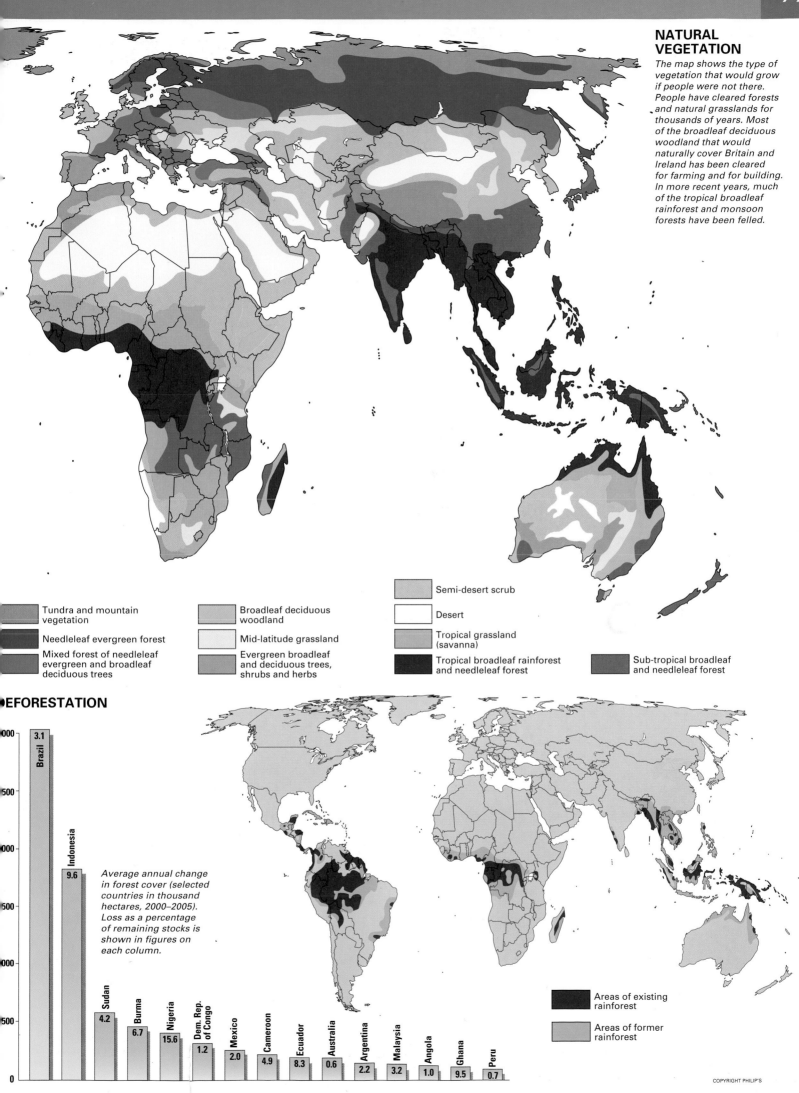

NATURAL VEGETATION

The map shows the type of vegetation that would grow if people were not there. People have cleared forests and natural grasslands for thousands of years. Most of the broadleaf deciduous woodland that would naturally cover Britain and Ireland has been cleared for farming and for building. In more recent years, much of the tropical broadleaf rainforest and monsoon forests have been felled.

Tundra and mountain vegetation

Needleleaf evergreen forest

Mixed forest of needleleaf evergreen and broadleaf deciduous trees

Broadleaf deciduous woodland

Mid-latitude grassland

Evergreen broadleaf and deciduous trees, shrubs and herbs

Semi-desert scrub

Desert

Tropical grassland (savanna)

Tropical broadleaf rainforest and needleleaf forest

Sub-tropical broadleaf and needleleaf forest

DEFORESTATION

Average annual change in forest cover (selected countries in thousand hectares, 2000–2005). Loss as a percentage of remaining stocks is shown in figures on each column.

Brazil	3.1
Indonesia	9.6
Sudan	4.2
Burma	6.7
Nigeria	15.6
Dem. Rep. of Congo	1.2
Mexico	2.0
Cameroon	4.9
Ecuador	8.3
Australia	0.6
Argentina	2.2
Malaysia	3.2
Angola	1.0
Ghana	9.5
Peru	0.7

Areas of existing rainforest

Areas of former rainforest

COPYRIGHT PHILIP'S

CONTINENTAL DRIFT

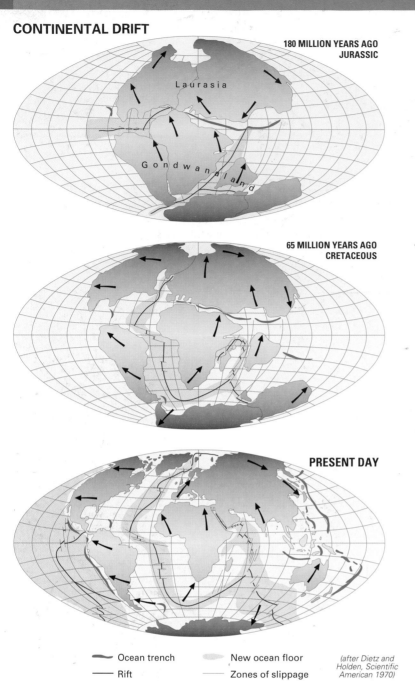

**180 MILLION YEARS AGO
JURASSIC**

Laurasia

Gondwanaland

**65 MILLION YEARS AGO
CRETACEOUS**

PRESENT DAY

—— Ocean trench   New ocean floor
—— Rift   —— Zones of slippage

*(after Dietz and
Holden, Scientific
American 1970)*

▲ In 1995, after almost 400 years lying dormant, the
Soufrière Hills volcano began a series of eruptions.
Further eruptions in 1996 and 1997 left the south of
the island uninhabitable and 5,000 people had to be
evacuated to the northern zone.

SOUFRIÈRE HILLS VOLCANO, MONTSERRAT

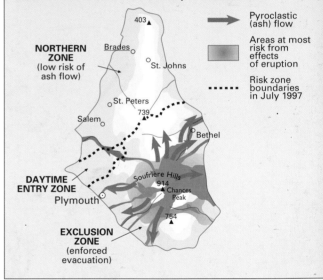

403 ▲

Brades

○ St. Johns

**NORTHERN
ZONE**
(low risk of
ash flow)

○ St. Peters
739

Salem ○

● Bethel

Soufrière Hills
914 ▲
Chances
Peak

**DAYTIME
ENTRY ZONE**
Plymouth ○

**EXCLUSION
ZONE**
(enforced
evacuation)

754 ▲

→ Pyroclastic
(ash) flow

Areas at most
risk from
effects
of eruption

······ Risk zone
boundaries
in July 1997

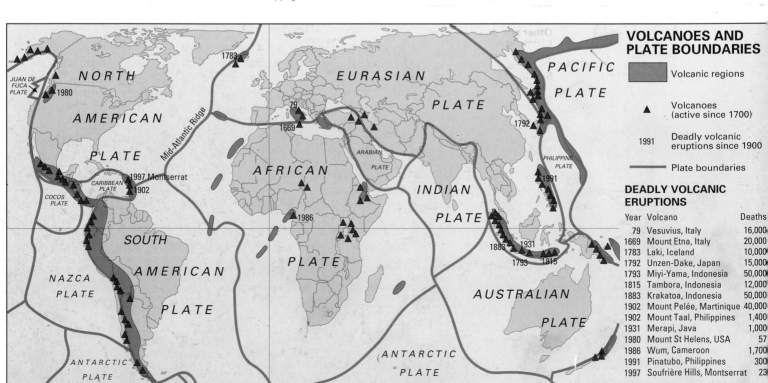

NORTH

JUAN DE
FUCA
PLATE

1980

AMERICAN

PLATE

1783

EURASIAN

PLATE

PACIFIC

PLATE

Mid-Atlantic Ridge

79

1669

1792

ARABIAN
PLATE

AFRICAN

PHILIPPINE
PLATE

1991

1997 Montserrat

CARIBBEAN
PLATE

1902

COCOS
PLATE

PLATE

INDIAN

PLATE

SOUTH

1986

AMERICAN

1883   1931

NAZCA
PLATE

PLATE

PLATE

1793   1815

AUSTRALIAN

PLATE

ANTARCTIC
PLATE

ANTARCTIC
PLATE

COPYRIGHT PHILIP'S

VOLCANOES AND
PLATE BOUNDARIES

▨ Volcanic regions

▲ Volcanoes
(active since 1700)

1991 Deadly volcanic
eruptions since 1900

—— Plate boundaries

DEADLY VOLCANIC
ERUPTIONS

Year	Volcano	Deaths
79	Vesuvius, Italy	16,000
1669	Mount Etna, Italy	20,000
1783	Laki, Iceland	10,000
1792	Unzen-Dake, Japan	15,000
1793	Miyi-Yama, Indonesia	50,000
1815	Tambora, Indonesia	12,000
1883	Krakatoa, Indonesia	50,000
1902	Mount Pelée, Martinique	40,000
1902	Mount Taal, Philippines	1,400
1931	Merapi, Java	1,000
1980	Mount St Helens, USA	57
1986	Wum, Cameroon	1,700
1991	Pinatubo, Philippines	300
1997	Soufrière Hills, Montserrat	23

PLATE TECTONICS IN THE CARIBBEAN

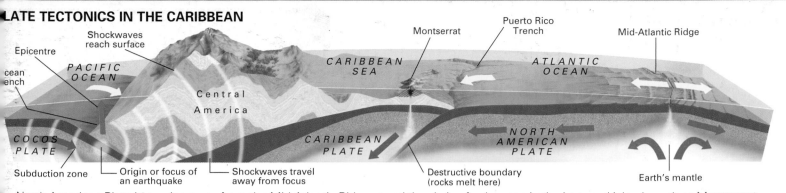

The North American Plate is moving away from the Mid-Atlantic Ridge and towards the Caribbean Plate at a rate of 30–40mm a year. The edge of the North American Plate is forced downwards under the Caribbean Plate. As the North American Plate descends, the rocks melt and are destroyed. This is called a *destructive boundary*. The destructive boundary to the east of the Caribbean has caused the Puerto Rico Trench and the chain of volcanoes in the Leeward Islands such as Montserrat. The molten rocks along the destructive boundary are forced upwards through cracks at the edge of the Caribbean Plate to pour out as lava from volcanoes. Earthquakes are also common along destructive plate boundaries, as is the case in Central America, along the boundary between the Caribbean and Cocos Plates.

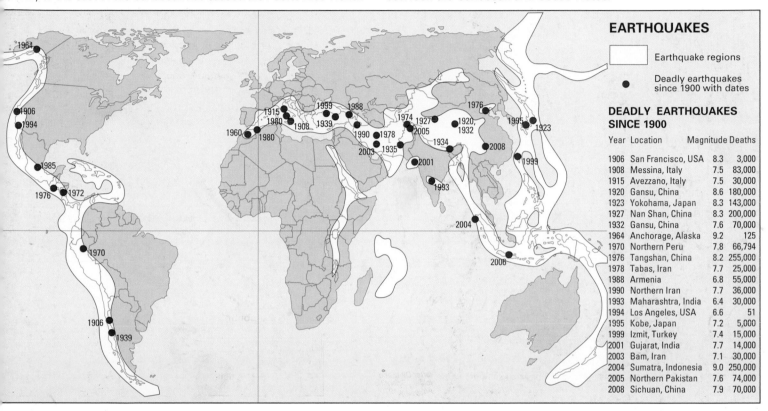

EARTHQUAKES

- Earthquake regions
- • Deadly earthquakes since 1900 with dates

DEADLY EARTHQUAKES SINCE 1900

Year	Location	Magnitude	Deaths
1906	San Francisco, USA	8.3	3,000
1908	Messina, Italy	7.5	83,000
1915	Avezzano, Italy	7.5	30,000
1920	Gansu, China	8.6	180,000
1923	Yokohama, Japan	8.3	143,000
1927	Nan Shan, China	8.3	200,000
1932	Gansu, China	7.6	70,000
1964	Anchorage, Alaska	9.2	125
1970	Northern Peru	7.8	66,794
1976	Tangshan, China	8.2	255,000
1978	Tabas, Iran	7.7	25,000
1988	Armenia	6.8	55,000
1990	Northern Iran	7.7	36,000
1993	Maharashtra, India	6.4	30,000
1994	Los Angeles, USA	6.6	51
1995	Kobe, Japan	7.2	5,000
1999	Izmit, Turkey	7.4	15,000
2001	Gujarat, India	7.7	14,000
2003	Bam, Iran	7.1	30,000
2004	Sumatra, Indonesia	9.0	250,000
2005	Northern Pakistan	7.6	74,000
2008	Sichuan, China	7.9	70,000

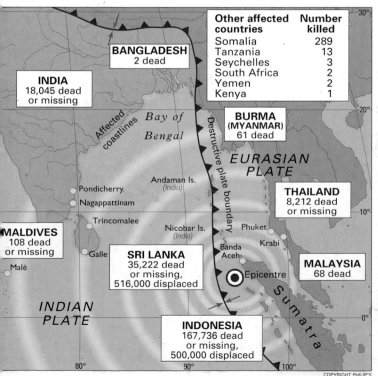

Other affected countries	Number killed
Somalia	289
Tanzania	13
Seychelles	3
South Africa	2
Yemen	2
Kenya	1

INDIAN OCEAN TSUNAMI

On 26 December 2004, an earthquake off the coast of Sumatra triggered a deadly tsunami that swept across the Indian Ocean, causing devastation in many countries (see map left).

The image below shows the turbulent receding waters of the tsunami, on the west coast of Sri Lanka. Such imagery enabled rescuers to assess the worst affected areas.

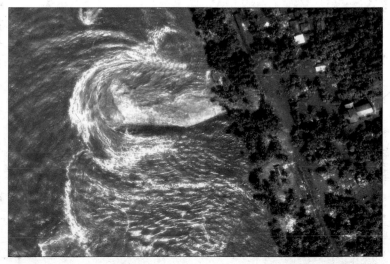

COPYRIGHT PHILIP'S

POPULATION DENSITY BY COUNTRY

Density of people per square kilometre (2006)

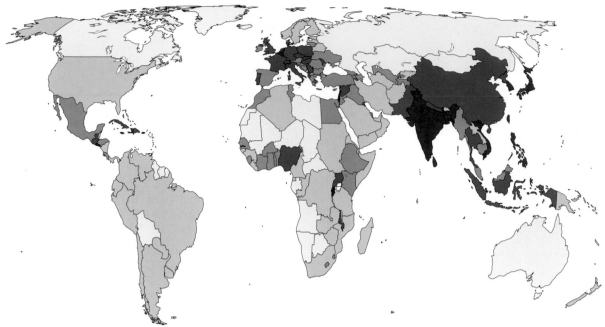

	250 per km² and over
	100 – 250 per km²
	50 – 100 per km²
	10 – 50 per km²
	Under 10 per km²
	No data

Most and least densely populated countries

Most per km²		Least per km²	
Monaco	16,689	W. Sahara	1.0
Singapore	6,482	Mongolia	1.8
Gaza Strip	3,969	Namibia	2.5
Malta	1,267	Australia	2.6
Maldives	1,197	Suriname	2.7

UK 247.6 per km²

POPULATION CHANGE

Expected change in total population (2000–2010)

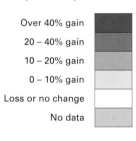

	Over 40% gain
	20 – 40% gain
	10 – 20% gain
	0 – 10% gain
	Loss or no change
	No data

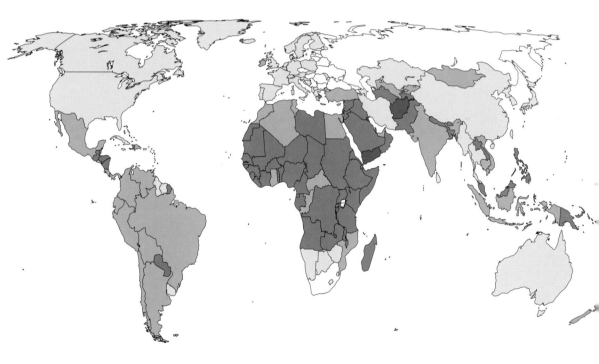

Countries with the greatest population gains and losses (%)

Greatest gains		Greatest losses	
Afghanistan	44.4	Bulgaria	−8.6
Kuwait	41.2	Trinidad & Tob.	−7.4
Yemen	41.0	Latvia	−6.7
Uganda	39.8	Estonia	−6.4
Oman	39.1	Ukraine	−6.1

UK 3% gain

URBAN POPULATION

Percentage of total population living in towns and cities (2005)

	80% urban and over
	60 – 80% urban
	40 – 60% urban
	20 – 40% urban
	Under 20% urban
	No data

Countries that are the most and least urbanized (%)

Most urbanized		Least urbanized	
Singapore	100	Burundi	10
Kuwait	97	Bhutan	11
Belgium	97	Trinidad & Tob.	12

UK 89.6

In 2008, for the first time in history, more than half the world's population lived in urban areas.

POPULATION BY CONTINENT

In this diagram the size of each continent is in proportion to its population.

Each square represents 10 million people.

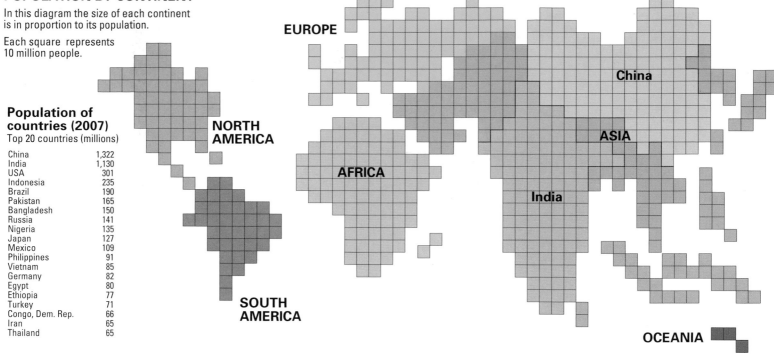

EUROPE

NORTH AMERICA

China

ASIA

AFRICA

India

SOUTH AMERICA

OCEANIA

Population of countries (2007)

Top 20 countries (millions)

China	1,322
India	1,130
USA	301
Indonesia	235
Brazil	190
Pakistan	165
Bangladesh	150
Russia	141
Nigeria	135
Japan	127
Mexico	109
Philippines	91
Vietnam	85
Germany	82
Egypt	80
Ethiopia	77
Turkey	71
Congo, Dem. Rep.	66
Iran	65
Thailand	65

LIFE EXPECTANCY

The average expected lifespan of babies born in 2007

- Over 75 years
- 65 – 75 years
- 55 – 65 years
- 45 – 55 years
- Under 45 years
- No data

Highest life expectancy (years)		Lowest life expectancy (years)	
Andorra	83.5	Mozambique	36.5
San Marino	81.2	Botswana	37.1
Japan	80.8	Zimbabwe	37.1
Singapore	80.2	Zambia	37.3
Australia	79.9	Angola	38.6

UK 78.7 years

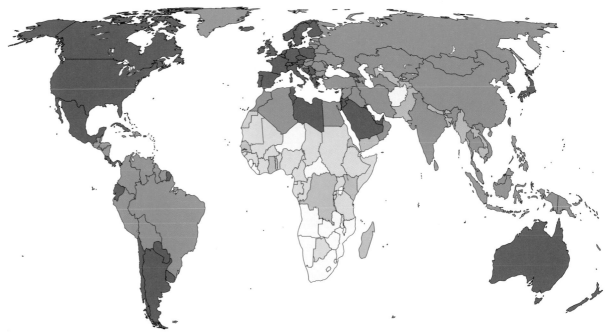

WEALTH

The value of total production in 2007 divided by the population (the Gross Domestic Product per capita)

- Over 250% of world average
- 100 – 250% of world average

World average wealth per person $10,000

- 50 – 100% of world average
- 15 – 50% of world average
- Under 15% of world average
- No data

Top 5 countries		Bottom 5 countries	
Luxembourg	$80,800	Congo (D. Rep.)	$300
Norway	$55,600	Liberia	$500
Kuwait	$55,300	Zimbabwe	$500
UAE	$55,200	Comoros	$600
Singapore	$48,900	Guinea-Bissau	$600

UK $35,000

ENERGY PRODUCTION

Energy produced
(in tonnes of oil equivalent)
per person (2007)

- Over 10 tonnes per person
- 1 – 10 tonnes per person
- 0.5 – 1 tonnes per person
- 0.1 – 0.5 tonnes per person
- Under 0.1 tonnes per person

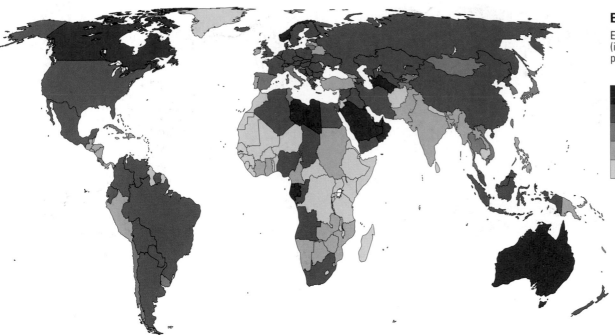

OIL RESERVES

World oil reserves by region and
country, thousand million tonnes (2006)

Abbreviations used:

Al:	Algeria	**No:**	Norway
Au:	Australia	**Po:**	Poland
Br:	Brazil	**Ru:**	Russia
Cn:	China	**SA:**	Saudi Arabia
In:	Indonesia	**S Af:**	South Africa
Iq:	Iraq	**UAE:**	United Arab Emirates
Ka:	Kazakhstan	**Uk:**	Ukraine
Li:	Libya	**USA:**	United States of America
Ni:	Nigeria	**Ve:**	Venezuela

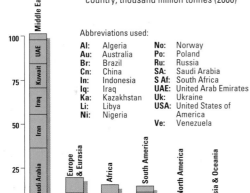

Saudi Arabia 13.1% · Russia 12.3% · USA 8.0% · Iran 5.4% · China 4.7% · Mexico 4.1% · Canada 3.9% · Venezuela 3.1% · Norway 3.3%

Oil production

World total (2006): 3,914,000,000 tonnes

GAS RESERVES

World natural gas reserves by
region and country, thousand
million tonnes of oil
equivalent (2006)

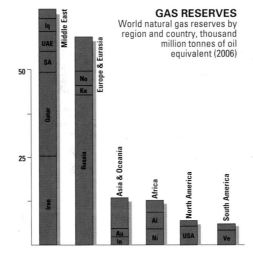

Russia 21.3% · USA 18.5% · Canada 6.5% · Iran 3.7% · Norway 3.1% · Algeria 2.9% · UK 2.6%

Gas production

World total (2006): 2,586,400,000 tonnes of oil equivalent

COAL RESERVES

World coal reserves by region
and country, thousand million
tonnes (2006, including lignite)

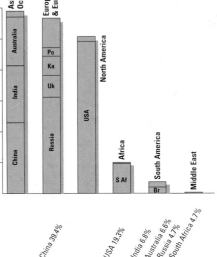

China 39.4% · USA 19.3% · India 6.8% · Australia 6.6% · Russia 4.7% · South Africa 4.7%

Coal production

World total (2006, excluding lignite): 3,079,700,000 tonnes

ENERGY CONSUMPTION

Primary energy consumption
(in tonnes of oil equivalent)
per person (2007)

- Over 10 tonnes per person
- 1 – 10 tonnes per person
- 0.5 – 1 tonnes per person
- 0.1 – 0.5 tonnes per person
- Under 0.1 tonnes per person

Countries consuming the most energy
(in tonnes of oil equivalent per person)

Virgin Islands	49
Qatar	25
UAE	23
Bahrain	17
Trinidad & Tobago	15

UK 4.1

FOOD PRODUCTION

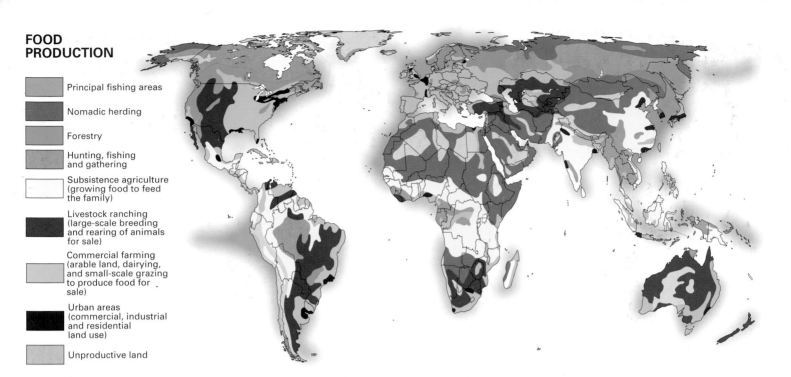

- Principal fishing areas
- Nomadic herding
- Forestry
- Hunting, fishing and gathering
- Subsistence agriculture (growing food to feed the family)
- Livestock ranching (large-scale breeding and rearing of animals for sale)
- Commercial farming (arable land, dairying, and small-scale grazing to produce food for sale)
- Urban areas (commercial, industrial and residential land use)
- Unproductive land

DAILY FOOD CONSUMPTION

Average daily food intake in calories per person (2003)

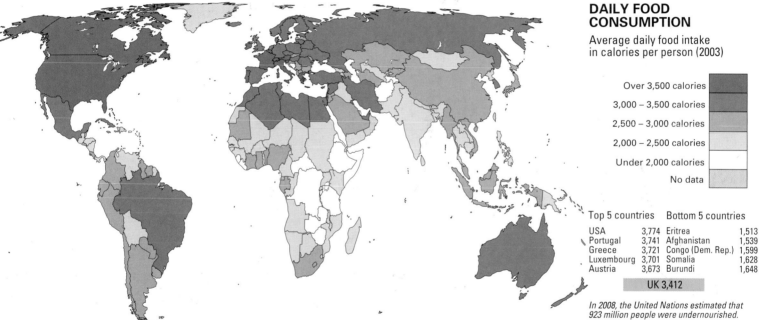

- Over 3,500 calories
- 3,000 – 3,500 calories
- 2,500 – 3,000 calories
- 2,000 – 2,500 calories
- Under 2,000 calories
- No data

Top 5 countries		Bottom 5 countries	
USA	3,774	Eritrea	1,513
Portugal	3,741	Afghanistan	1,539
Greece	3,721	Congo (Dem. Rep.)	1,599
Luxembourg	3,701	Somalia	1,628
Austria	3,673	Burundi	1,648

UK 3,412

In 2008, the United Nations estimated that 923 million people were undernourished.

WATER SUPPLY

The percentage of total population with access to safe drinking water (2004)

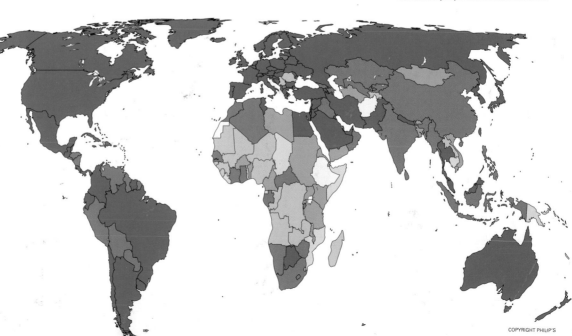

- Over 90% with safe water
- 75 – 90% with safe water
- 60 – 75% with safe water
- 45 – 60% with safe water
- 30 – 45% with safe water
- Under 30% with safe water

Least well-provided countries

Afghanistan	13%
Ethiopia	22%
Western Sahara	26%
Papua New Guinea	39%
Cambodia	41%
Somalia	42%

One person in eight in the world has no access to a safe water supply.

WORLD TRADE

The percentage share of total
world exports by value (2007)

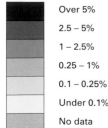

	Over 5%
	2.5 – 5%
	1 – 2.5%
	0.25 – 1%
	0.1 – 0.25%
	Under 0.1%
	No data
☆	Member of 'G8'

*The members of 'G8' account
for more than half the total trade.
The majority of nations contribute
less than one quarter of 1% to
the worldwide total of exports;
EU countries account for 35%; the
Pacific Rim nations over 50%.*

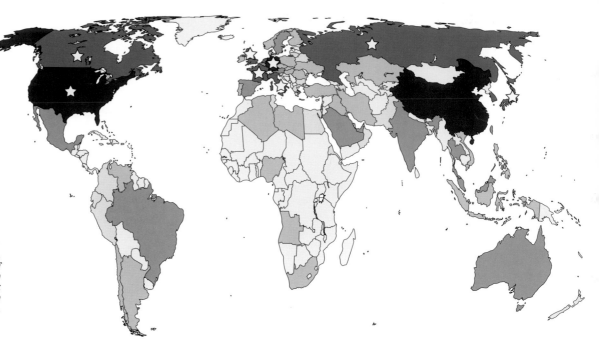

INTERNET USERS

The percentage of
total population
using the internet (2007)

	Over 50% use the internet
	25 – 50% use the internet
	10 – 25% use the internet
	1 – 10% use the internet
	Under 1% use the internet
	No data

Top 5 countries		Bottom 5 countries	
Netherlands	91%	East Timor	0.1%
Antigua & B.	86%	Burma	0.1%
Canada	84%	Sierra Leone	0.2%
Norway	82%	Iraq	0.2%
Andorra	82%	Niger	0.3%
	UK 66%		

INTERNATIONAL AID

Official Development
Assistance (ODA) provided
and received, US$ per
capita (2007)

	Over $100
	$50 – $100
	$20 – $50

PROVIDERS ↑

	Under $10
	$10 – $25
	$25 – $50
	Over $50
	No data

RECEIVERS ↓

Top 5 providers		Top 5 receivers	
Norway	$638	Nauru	$1,478
Luxembourg	$606	Micronesia	$983
Sweden	$438	Tuvalu	$834
Denmark	$408	Iraq	$787
Netherlands	$329	Lebanon	$764
UK provides $205			

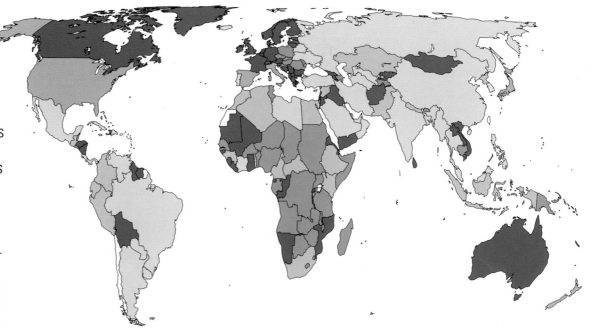

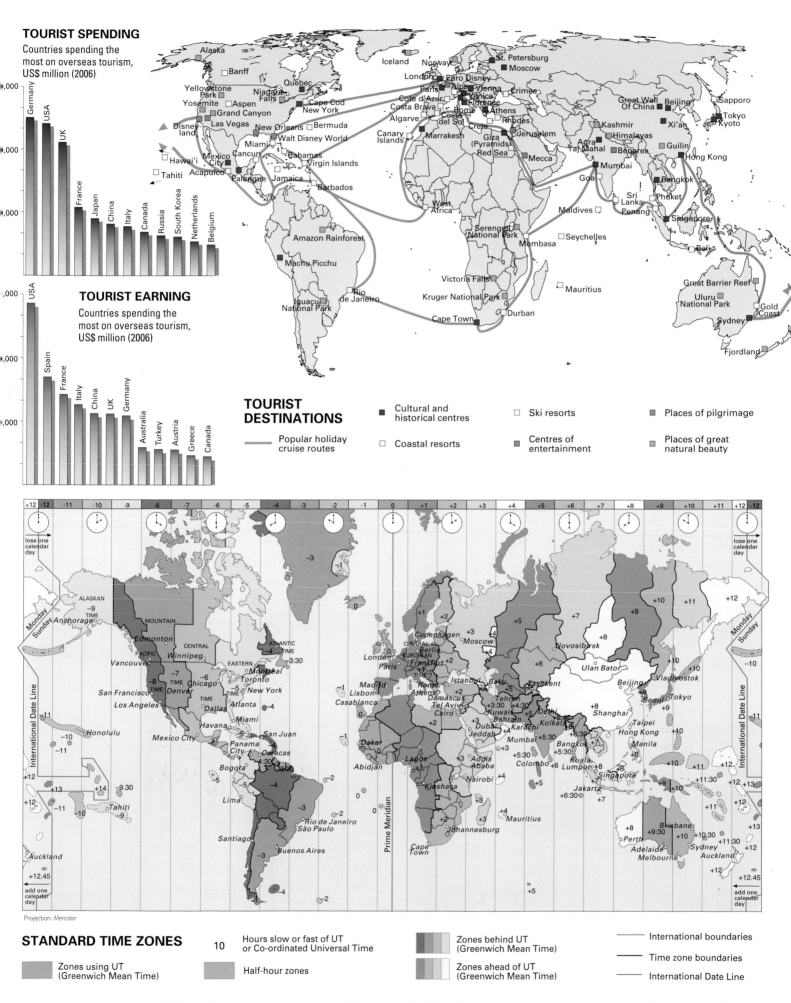

TOURIST SPENDING

Countries spending the most on overseas tourism, US$ million (2006)

Bar chart (US$ million): Germany, USA, UK, France, Japan, China, Italy, Canada, Russia, South Korea, Netherlands, Belgium

TOURIST EARNING

Countries spending the most on overseas tourism, US$ million (2006)

Bar chart (US$ million): USA, Spain, France, Italy, China, UK, Germany, Australia, Turkey, Austria, Greece, Canada

TOURIST DESTINATIONS

- ■ Cultural and historical centres
- □ Coastal resorts
- ── Popular holiday cruise routes
- □ Ski resorts
- ■ Centres of entertainment
- ■ Places of pilgrimage
- ■ Places of great natural beauty

STANDARD TIME ZONES

Projection: Mercator

10   Hours slow or fast of UT or Co-ordinated Universal Time

- ■ Zones using UT (Greenwich Mean Time)
- Half-hour zones
- ▨ Zones behind UT (Greenwich Mean Time)
- ▨ Zones ahead of UT (Greenwich Mean Time)
- ---- International boundaries
- ── Time zone boundaries
- ── International Date Line

The Earth rotates through 360° in 24 hours, and so moves 15° every hour. The World is divided into 24 standard time zones, each centred on lines of longitude at 15° intervals. The Greenwich Meridian (or Prime Meridian) lies on the centre of the first zone. All places to the west of Greenwich are one hour behind for every 15° of longitude; places to the east are ahead by one hour for every 15°.

FLAG	COUNTRY	CAPITAL CITY	AREA thousand square kilometres 2007	POPULATION million people 2007	POPULATION CHANGE percent per year 2007	BIRTHS per thousand people 2007	DEATHS per thousand people 2007	LIFE EXPECTANCY years 2007	INCOME US$ per person 2007
	Afghanistan	Kabul	652	31.9	2.6	46	20	44	800
	Albania	Tirane	28.7	3.6	0.5	15	5	78	5,500
	Algeria	Algiers	2,382	33.3	1.2	17	5	74	8,100
	Angola	Luanda	1,247	12.3	2.2	44	24	34	6,500
	Argentina	Buenos Aires	2,780	40.3	0.9	18	7	76	13,000
	Armenia	Yerevan	29.8	3.0	-0.1	13	8	72	5,700
	Australia	Canberra	7,741	20.4	0.8	13	7	82	37,500
	Austria	Vienna	83.9	8.2	0.1	9	10	79	39,000
	Azerbaijan	Baku	86.6	8.1	0.7	18	8	66	9,000
	Bahamas	Nassau	13.9	0.3	0.6	17	9	66	22,700
	Bahrain	Manama	0.69	0.7	1.4	17	4	75	34,700
	Bangladesh	Dhaka	144	150.4	2.1	29	8	63	1,400
	Barbados	Bridgetown	0.43	0.3	0.4	12	9	73	19,700
	Belarus	Minsk	208	9.7	-0.4	10	14	70	10,200
	Belgium	Brussels	30.5	10.4	0.1	10	10	79	36,500
	Belize	Belmopan	23	0.3	2.3	28	6	68	7,800
	Benin	Porto-Novo	113	8.1	2.7	40	10	59	1,500
	Bhutan	Thimphu	47	2.3	2.1	21	8	66	1,400
	Bolivia	La Paz/Sucre	1,099	9.1	1.4	22	7	67	4,400
	Bosnia-Herzegovina	Sarajevo	51.2	4.6	1.0	9	9	78	6,600
	Botswana	Gaborone	582	1.8	1.5	23	14	50	14,700
	Brazil	Brasília	8,514	190.0	1.0	19	6	72	9,700
	Brunei	Bandar Seri Begawan	5.8	0.4	1.8	18	3	76	25,600
	Bulgaria	Sofia	111	7.3	-0.8	10	14	73	11,800
	Burkina Faso	Ouagadougou	274	14.3	3.0	45	14	53	1,200
	Burma (Myanmar)	Rangoon/Naypyidaw	677	47.4	0.8	17	9	63	1,900
	Burundi	Bujumbura	27.8	8.4	3.6	42	13	52	800
	Cambodia	Phnom Penh	181	14.0	1.7	26	8	62	1,800
	Cameroon	Yaoundé	475	18.1	2.2	35	12	53	2,300
	Canada	Ottawa	9,971	33.4	0.9	10	8	81	38,200
	Cape Verde Islands	Praia	4	0.4	0.6	24	6	71	7,000
	Central African Republic	Bangui	623	4.4	1.5	33	18	44	700
	Chad	N'djamena	1,284	9.9	2.3	42	16	47	1,600
	Chile	Santiago	757	16.3	0.9	15	6	77	14,400
	China	Beijing	9,597	1,321.9	0.6	14	7	73	5,300
	Colombia	Bogotá	1,139	44.4	1.4	20	6	73	7,200
	Comoros	Moroni	2.2	0.7	2.8	36	8	63	600
	Congo	Brazzaville	342	3.8	2.6	42	12	54	3,700
	Congo (Dem. Rep.)	Kinshasa	2,345	65.8	3.4	43	12	54	300
	Costa Rica	San José	51.1	4.1	1.4	18	4	77	13,500
	Croatia	Zagreb	56.5	4.5	0.0	10	12	75	15,500
	Cuba	Havana	111	11.4	0.3	11	7	77	4,500
	Cyprus	Nicosia	9.3	0.8	0.5	13	8	78	24,600

FLAG	COUNTRY	CAPITAL CITY	AREA thousand square kilometres 2007	POPULATION million people 2007	POPULATION CHANGE percent per year 2007	BIRTHS per thousand people 2007	DEATHS per thousand people 2007	LIFE EXPECTANCY years 2007	INCOME US$ per person 2007
	Czech Republic	Prague	78.9	10.2	-0.1	9	11	77	24,400
	Denmark	Copenhagen	43.1	5.5	0.3	11	10	78	37,400
	Djibouti	Djibouti	23.2	0.5	2.0	39	19	43	1,000
	Dominican Republic	Santo Domingo	48.5	9.4	1.5	23	5	73	9,200
	East Timor	Dili	14.9	1.1	2.1	27	6	67	800
	Ecuador	Quito	284	13.8	1.6	22	4	77	7,100
	Egypt	Cairo	1,001	80.3	1.7	22	5	72	5,400
	El Salvador	San Salvador	21	6.9	1.7	26	6	72	5,200
	Equatorial Guinea	Malabo	28.1	0.6	2.0	37	10	61	4,100
	Eritrea	Asmara	118	4.9	2.5	35	9	61	1,000
	Estonia	Tallinn	45.1	1.3	-0.6	10	13	73	21,800
	Ethiopia	Addis Ababa	1,104	76.5	2.3	44	12	55	700
	Fiji	Suva	18.3	0.9	1.4	22	6	70	4,100
	Finland	Helsinki	338	5.2	0.1	10	10	79	35,500
	France	Paris	552	60.9	0.6	13	8	81	33,800
	Gabon	Libreville	268	1.5	2.0	36	13	54	13,800
	Gambia	Banjul	11.3	1.7	2.8	38	12	55	800
	Georgia	Tbilisi	69.7	4.6	-0.3	11	10	77	4,200
	Germany	Berlin	357	82.4	0.0	8	11	79	34,400
	Ghana	Accra	239	22.9	2.0	29	9	59	1,400
	Greece	Athens	132	10.7	0.2	10	10	80	30,500
	Guatemala	Guatemala	109	12.7	2.2	29	5	70	5,400
	Guinea	Conakry	246	9.9	2.6	38	11	57	1,000
	Guinea-Bissau	Bissau	36.1	1.5	2.1	36	16	48	600
	Guyana	Georgetown	215	0.8	0.2	18	8	66	5,300
	Haiti	Port-au-Prince	27.8	8.7	2.5	36	10	58	1,900
	Honduras	Tegucigalpa	112	7.5	2.1	27	5	69	3,300
	Hungary	Budapest	93	10.0	-0.3	10	13	73	19,500
	Iceland	Reykjavik	103	0.3	0.8	14	7	81	39,400
	India	New Delhi	3,287	1129.9	1.6	22	6	69	2,700
	Indonesia	Jakarta	1,905	234.7	1.2	19	6	70	3,400
	Iran	Tehrān	1,648	65.4	0.7	17	6	71	12,300
	Iraq	Baghdād	438	27.5	2.6	31	5	70	3,600
	Ireland	Dublin	70.3	4.1	1.1	14	8	78	45,600
	Israel	Jerusalem	20.6	6.4	1.2	20	5	81	28,800
	Italy	Rome	301	58.1	0.0	8	11	80	31,000
	Ivory Coast	Yamoussoukro	322	18.0	2.0	33	11	55	1,800
	Jamaica	Kingston	11	2.8	0.8	20	6	74	4,800
	Japan	Tōkyō	378	127.4	-0.1	8	9	82	33,800
	Jordan	Amman	89.3	6.1	2.4	20	3	79	4,700
	Kazakhstan	Astana	2,725	15.3	0.4	16	9	68	11,100
	Kenya	Nairobi	580	36.9	2.8	38	10	57	1,600
	Korea, North	P'yŏngyang	121	23.3	0.8	15	7	72	1,900

FLAG	COUNTRY	CAPITAL CITY	AREA thousand square kilometres 2007	POPULATION million people 2007	POPULATION CHANGE percent per year 2000–2007	BIRTHS per thousand people 2007	DEATHS per thousand people 2007	LIFE EXPECTANCY years 2007	INCOME US$ per person 2007
	Korea, South	Seoul	99.3	49.0	0.4	9	6	79	24,600
	Kosovo	Priština	10.9	2.1					1,800
	Kuwait	Kuwait	17.8	2.5	3.6	22	2	78	55,300
	Kyrgyzstan	Bishkek	200	5.3	1.4	23	7	69	2,000
	Laos	Vientiane	237	6.5	2.4	34	11	56	1,900
	Latvia	Riga	64.6	2.3	-0.6	10	14	72	17,700
	Lebanon	Beirut	10.4	3.9	1.2	18	6	73	10,400
	Lesotho	Maseru	30.4	2.1	0.1	24	22	40	1,500
	Liberia	Monrovia	111	3.2	4.8	43	21	41	500
	Libya	Tripoli	1,760	6.0	2.3	26	3	77	13,100
	Lithuania	Vilnius	65.2	3.6	-0.3	9	11	75	16,700
	Luxembourg	Luxembourg	2.6	0.5	1.2	12	8	79	80,800
	Macedonia	Skopje	25.7	2.1	0.3	12	9	74	8,400
	Madagascar	Antananarivo	587	19.4	3.0	38	8	63	1,000
	Malawi	Lilongwe	118	13.6	2.4	42	18	43	800
	Malaysia	Kuala Lumpur/ Putrajaya	330	24.8	1.8	22	5	73	14,400
	Mali	Bamako	1,240	12.0	2.7	49	16	50	1,200
	Malta	Valletta	0.32	0.4	0.4	10	8	79	23,200
	Mauritania	Nouakchott	1,026	3.3	2.9	40	12	54	1,800
	Mauritius	Port Louis	2	1.3	0.8	15	7	74	11,900
	Mexico	Mexico	1,958	108.7	1.2	20	5	76	12,500
	Moldova	Chişinău	33.9	4.3	-0.1	11	11	71	2,200
	Mongolia	Ulan Bator	1,567	3.0	1.5	21	6	67	2,900
	Montenegro	Podgorica	14	0.7	-1.0	11	9		3,800
	Morocco	Rabat	447	33.8	1.5	21	5	72	3,800
	Mozambique	Maputo	802	20.9	1.8	38	20	41	900
	Namibia	Windhoek	824	2.1	0.5	23	14	50	5,200
	Nepal	Katmandu	147	28.9	2.1	30	9	61	1,100
	Netherlands	Amsterdam/ The Hague	41.5	16.6	0.5	11	9	79	38,600
	New Zealand	Wellington	271	4.1	1.0	14	7	80	27,300
	Nicaragua	Managua	130	5.7	1.9	24	4	71	3,200
	Niger	Niamey	1,267	12.9	2.9	50	20	44	700
	Nigeria	Abuja	924	135.0	2.4	37	17	47	2,200
	Norway	Oslo	324	4.6	0.4	11	9	80	55,600
	Oman	Muscat	310	3.2	3.2	35	4	74	19,100
	Pakistan	Islamabad	796	164.7	1.8	28	8	64	2,600
	Panama	Panamá	75.5	3.2	1.6	21	5	77	9,000
	Papua New Guinea	Port Moresby	463	5.8	2.2	28	7	66	2,900
	Paraguay	Asunción	407	6.7	2.4	28	4	76	4,000
	Peru	Lima	1,285	28.7	1.3	20	6	70	7,600
	Philippines	Manila	300	91.1	1.8	26	5	71	3,300
	Poland	Warsaw	323	38.5	0.0	10	10	75	16,200
	Portugal	Lisbon	88.8	10.6	0.3	10	11	78	21,800

FLAG	COUNTRY	CAPITAL CITY	AREA thousand square kilometres 2007	POPULATION million people 2007	POPULATION CHANGE percent per year 2007	BIRTHS per thousand people 2007	DEATHS per thousand people 2007	LIFE EXPECTANCY years 2007	INCOME US$ per person 2007
	Qatar	Doha	11	0.9	2.4	16	2	75	29,400
	Romania	Bucharest	238	22.3	-0.1	11	12	72	11,100
	Russia	Moscow	17,075	141.4	-0.5	11	16	66	14,600
	Rwanda	Kigali	26.3	9.9	2.8	40	14	50	1,000
	Saudi Arabia	Riyadh	2,150	27.6	2.1	29	2	76	20,700
	Senegal	Dakar	197	12.5	2.6	37	11	57	1,700
	Serbia	Belgrade	77.5	8.0				75	7,700
	Sierra Leone	Freetown	71.7	6.1	2.3	45	22	41	800
	Singapore	Singapore	0.68	4.6	1.3	9	5	82	48,900
	Slovakia	Bratislava	49	5.4	0.1	11	10	75	19,800
	Slovenia	Ljubljana	20.3	2.0	-0.1	9	11	77	27,300
	Solomon Islands	Honiara	28.9	0.6	2.5	28	4	73	600
	Somalia	Mogadishu	638	9.1	2.8	44	16	49	600
	South Africa	Cape Town/ Pretoria	1,221	44.0	-0.5	20	17	49	10,600
	Spain	Madrid	498	40.4	0.1	10	10	80	33,700
	Sri Lanka	Colombo	65.6	20.9	1.0	17	6	75	4,100
	Sudan	Khartoum	2,506	39.4	2.1	34	14	50	2,500
	Suriname	Paramaribo	163	0.5	1.1	17	6	73	7,800
	Swaziland	Mbabane	17.4	1.1	-0.3	27	31	32	4,800
	Sweden	Stockholm	450	9.0	0.2	10	10	81	36,900
	Switzerland	Berne	41.3	7.6	0.4	10	9	81	39,800
	Syria	Damascus	185	19.3	2.2	27	5	71	4,500
	Taiwan	Taipei	36	22.9	0.3	9	7	78	29,800
	Tajikistan	Dushanbe	143	7.1	1.9	27	7	65	1,600
	Tanzania	Dodoma	945	39.4	2.1	35	13	51	1,100
	Thailand	Bangkok	513	65.1	0.7	14	7	73	8,000
	Togo	Lomé	56.8	5.7	2.7	37	9	58	900
	Trinidad and Tobago	Port of Spain	5.1	1.1	-0.9	13	11	67	21,700
	Tunisia	Tunis	164	10.3	1.0	16	5	76	7,500
	Turkey	Ankara	775	71.2	1.0	16	6	73	9,400
	Turkmenistan	Ashkhabad	488	5.1	1.6	25	6	69	9,200
	Uganda	Kampala	241	30.3	3.6	48	12	52	1,100
	Ukraine	Kiev	604	46.3	-0.7	10	16	68	6,900
	United Arab Emirates	Abu Dhabi	83.6	4.4	4.0	16	2	76	55,200
	United Kingdom	London	242	60.8	0.3	11	10	79	35,300
	USA	Washington D.C.	9,629	301.1	0.9	14	8	78	46,000
	Uruguay	Montevideo	175	3.5	0.5	14	9	76	10,700
	Uzbekistan	Tashkent	447	27.8	1.7	18	5	72	2,200
	Venezuela	Caracas	912	26.0	1.5	21	5	73	12,800
	Vietnam	Hanoi	332	85.3	1.0	16	6	71	2,600
	Yemen	Sana	528	22.2	3.5	42	8	63	2,400
	Zambia	Lusaka	753	11.5	1.7	41	21	39	1,400
	Zimbabwe	Harare	391	12.3	0.6	32	17	44	500

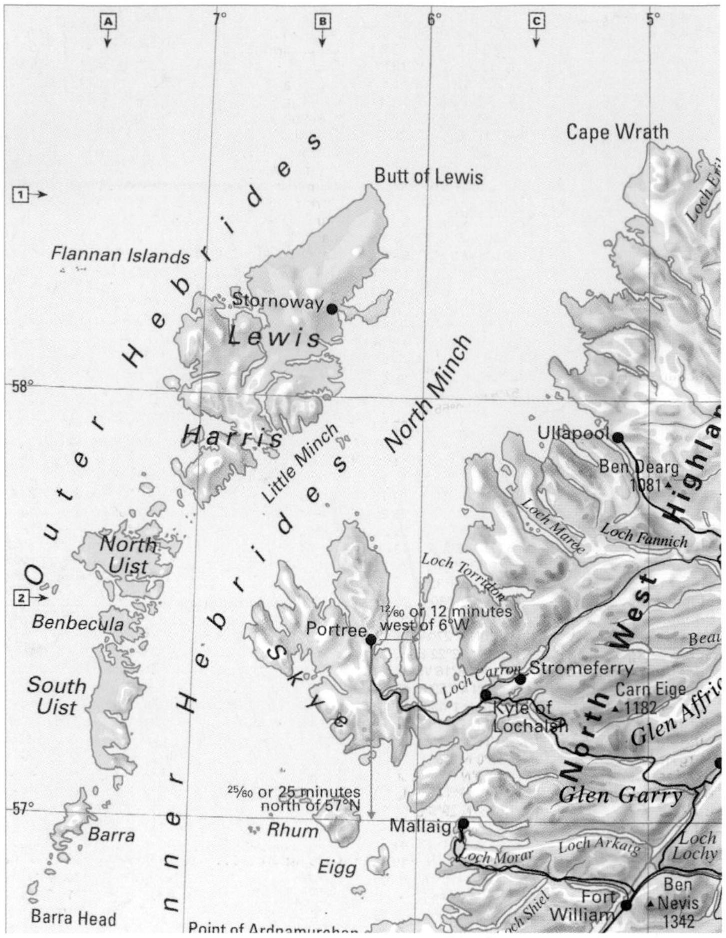

This index contains the names of all the principal places and features shown on the maps in the atlas. They are listed in alphabetical order. If a name has a description as part of it, for example, Bay of Biscay, the name is in alphabetical order, followed by the description:

Biscay, Bay of. . . . .

Sometimes, the same name occurs in more than one country. In these cases, the country names are added after each place name, and they are indexed alphabetically by that country.
For example:

Córdoba *Argentina* . . . . .
Córdoba *Spain* . . . .

All rivers are indexed to their mouths or confluences and are followed by the symbol ➙. All country names are followed by the symbol ■.

Each place name is followed by its latitude and longitude, and then its map page number and figure-letter grid reference. Both latitude and longitude are measured in degrees and minutes. There are 60 minutes in a degree. The latitude is followed by N(orth) or S(outh) and the longitude by E(ast) or W(est). The map extract on the left shows how to find a place by estimating the required distance from the nearest line of latitude or longitude on the map page. Portree is used as an example:

Portree . . . . 57°25′N 6°12′W **14 2B**

There are 60 minutes between the lines and so to find the position of Portree an estimate has to be made. 25 parts of the 60 minutes north of the 57°N latitude line, and 12 parts of the 60 minutes west of the 6°W longitude line. The latitude and longitude are followed by a number in bold type which refers to the number of the map page on which the place or feature appears.

The figure and letter which follow the page number give the grid rectangle on the map within which the place or feature appears. The grid is formed by the lines of latitude and longitude. The columns are labelled at the top and bottom with a letter and the rows at the sides with a number. Portree, for example, is in the grid square where row 2 crosses column B.